# God's
# Prickly Pear

# Yaffa

# GOD'S
# PRICKLY PEAR

Yaffa McPherson

Intimate Awe Publications

Published by
Intimate Awe Publications
P.O. Box 536
Hopedale, OH 43976

Typesetting, technical advice and production assistance:
White Stone Publishing
P.O. Box 35754
Des Moines, IA 50315

Printed in the United States of America

Library of Congress Catalog Card Number: 92-97176

ISBN  0-9634792-0-2

# About the Cover

In Israel, a native Jew is called *Sabra* (prickly pear). The Israeli-born is likened to the distinctive characteristics of this cactus fruit: a prickly exterior but a tender heart. Israel's need for natives in these early years as a nation produced an unwritten law saying that any Jewish child who speaks his first words and takes his first steps in Israel is a native. I was considered a *Sabra*.

Front cover design and drawing by Yaffa McPherson
Back cover design and photo by Ken McPherson

*My heartfelt gratitude*

*to Ken, my loving husband and best friend, who journeyed with me into my story and into my very thoughts, intensely involving himself with tireless hours of typing and helpful suggestions;*

*To "all" our children, some of whom relished reading bits and pieces as they were being put together and "cooperated" and prayed for its completion;*

*To friends who took interest in my story and were an encouragement to me.*

To protect anonymity,

some of the people's names have been changed.

# God's Prickly Pear

## CONTENTS

# *Earliest Recollections*

**I awaken in my rickety crib** in a corner of our one-room wooden shack discovering I am alone. Unlike other days, the shutters are closed. In the half-dark room, thin slivers of light peek through two cracks in a broken slat. I stand up in the crib and stare at the light slivers, waiting and waiting in the empty silence. No one coming home, I begin to cry. Then I scream, "Grandmother! Grandmo-o-the-er!" Hour after hour -- sitting, standing, lying down and then back on my feet again -- I keep screaming, "Grandmo-o-the-er!.." No response. My voice becoming weary, I stop screaming to sob. When I recover, I scream again. Still no one comes.

After some time, fright overtakes me and I resort to screaming louder, hoping to be heard outside. With my remaining strength I keep at it, begging for anyone's presence, to no avail. The light slivers disappear. I doze, then awaken in the dark and scream until I am dizzy with frenzy.

My throat is sore; my body is now weak. The thick layers of rags pinned on me in diaper fashion weigh heavy with wetness. I feel for a dry spot on my mattress. I itch and sting all over my body. I am too frightened and too tired to climb out of the crib. Wetter and hungrier, I scream myself to fretful naps. Light slivers are appearing and disappearing. Waking... screaming... dozing... Still no one comes. Waking, screaming and dozing, I am reaching the point when I no longer care about anything. Weaker and weaker, I just want to close my eyes.

Suddenly, I am jolted awake as the door comes crashing in. A policeman bursts through. Grandmother steps in, Father trailing behind. With renewed strength, I reach out for comfort, but none comes. The only words I hear are Grandmother's angry protests to the policeman. The only touch I feel on my wet body is the chilling breeze from the broken doorway...

I was not quite three when this happened to me, and scarcely remember the scandalous divorce that followed; the recurring nightmares of the abandonment overshadowed it. Along with the devastating effects of this crisis, I grew up tormented by Grandmother's explanation for why it happened. "Your lying, selfish mother abandoned you for three days. Who knows what would have happened if I hadn't rescued you!" Disappointed in my mother, I was grateful to Grandmother, and glad for the divorce.

I remember how viciously the neighbors condemned and mocked me. Divorce was a rare happening among Jews then -- a reproach deserving ostracism.

In those days we lived in the small town of Yaffo, the Biblical port of Joppa. We immigrated there from Europe in 1947, a year before Israel became a nation again. I was an infant then. As for my mother, I cannot recall her living with us, though she had.

Even before Grandmother took over, Father was serving in the Israeli Navy and was seldom home. His absence added to my distress. Grandmother offered no consolation for Father's absence. In fact, she was emphatically intolerant of me and of my constant jabbering. More often than not, she sent me away from her presence. At first, when she did that, I fled to my asphalt yard, the street. There I watched people -- Arabs and Jews -- passing our house. There was nowhere else for me to go when Grandmother shunned me in our one-room abode. When she was in that kind of mood, home wasn't *my* home. Eventually, I ventured off, barefoot and wearing ill-fitting clothes, to play with the Arab children in our slum. Our street sloped down toward the muddy, abandoned seaport, and if I stood tall enough, I could see the ocean in the distance. I avoided venturing that direction, for the ocean frightened me. Rather, I chose to walk uphill to play. All I had to play with, in the house or out, were my thoughts. Contemplation became the dominant pastime in my life.

I was only four when Grandmother determined to send me to kindergarten. I dreaded the prospect. Were it not for her unyielding grip on my bony wrist when she took me to school that morning, I would have darted back home. One stern look from the school registrar was enough to crush me. It sent me miles away emotionally. Still unable to wriggle out of Grandmother's grip, I cowered.

"May I see her birth certificate, please?" she asked in broken German, after Grandmother's apology for speaking no Hebrew.

"I'm sorry, we just haven't gotten around to sending for it from Germany. Surely you can understand that after all I went through in Europe, I had not had the nerve to write there. We purposely carried no birth certificate when Yaffa was born. We were planning our illegal escape and she was concealed."

My personal predicament was twofold. Since Grandmother took over, I had picked up German, the language she used at home with Father. I was thought to know only Hungarian. Mentally, I was way ahead of my emotions and I understood too much for my own welfare.

Lack of proof for my age brought immediate prejudice between the obviously Israeli-born young registrar and my impatient European Grandmother of odd behavior. The tension in their voices frightened me. When Grandmother needed both of her hands to speak with emotion, I took full advantage. Instantly, I slipped away and, choosing a far corner, I seated myself on the floor. Thumb in mouth, I listened intently as the registrar spoke with suppressed aggravation.

"We cannot accept your verbal claim that she is five," assured the registrar. "Look how she behaves -- like a two year-old. She would have difficulties with other children at this time. Perhaps next year..."

"No!" Grandmother pounded the desk, "I want her in school now!" I snapped my thumb out of my mouth and cringed.

"But without documents she cannot attend public school. Legally, she does not exist. We will be glad to help you send for the certificate if you give us... just a moment... please don't leave..."

4

Grandmother whisked me out of the corner and I skated out the door behind her, still processing in my mind the registrar's cruel comments. How devastating it was to hear that I appeared like a two-year old, even though I was not yet five, as Grandmother claimed.

I never knew she could walk so fast. We raced downhill, her fingers biting into my arm. Fear gripped my heart as I ran, now and then leaping, to keep up with her. I dared not slow down my overworked legs, else be dragged along like a rag doll. She wasn't about to slow down for me. Wherever she was taking me, she was in an awful hurry to get there.

*The seaport! How could she?* I broke into tears, staring at waves as angry as I knew Grandmother was. Escape was impossible. *My end is coming...* I closed my eyes.

Grandmother's heavy, labored breathing finally slowed her down but did not stop her. Instead, she gave my weary, aching arm a disgusted jerk, and we turned onto a side street. I snapped out of my dejected thoughts, and gratefully decided that she was not going to throw me into the ocean. In a moment, I found myself entering the doors of a strange, dingy little office. A nun in black sat behind an old, battered desk. She greeted us with a silent, religious nod.

I'd heard about the "haunted" convent from Arab neighbor children, and was sorely afraid of those nuns. We children, Arab and Jewish alike, superstitiously kept our distance from these dreaded "creatures." Seeing no hands, no feet, and no neck, their covered heads looked unattached. To us they were ghosts. Their pasty-white faces seemed to float atop the masses of black clothing. It was the kind of thing we tan-faced children dared one another to stare at from afar. Then we bolted home with pounding hearts.

An eery shiver attacked my little body when I heard Grandmother speaking an unfamiliar language.

*She's going to let the spooky foreign nuns keep me and I'll never return home.*

Next I was led down to a musty green-walled room at the bottom of a long flight of stairs. There, another pasty-white face stared at me. For the first time I realized it had eyes, nose and mouth. The mouth opened and the "creature" spoke to me. Petrified, my own mouth froze shut, my eyes searching for Grandmother... She was gone.

Crying, I refused to let the "creature" touch me, so I merely stumbled forward in the direction it wished me to go. We entered a dungeon-like musty classroom. *Would I end up looking like a ghost?* I wondered, as I was led to a seat and handed a book.

It wasn't until that afternoon, when I was sent home, that I realized I had been enrolled in the convent school. Grandmother said not a word about the school when I arrived home. Neither did I. Her silence spoke the loud message to me that she was not going to change her mind.

Unheard of! Entering Catholic grounds was considered a grave sin by most Jews. By the Arab (Moslem) children it was a curse, and by me it was cruel punishment. For my grandmother, who had no regard for religion or for me, the convent was her perfect means of retaliation. It mattered not to her that I was, expectedly, the only Jewish child there; neither did it matter what a religious double standard would do to me.

I was sure Father would have never considered a non-

Jewish school. He used to tell my older brother, Mischa, "Never be ashamed that you are a Jew." How hypocritical I felt on the way to school each day, but I dared not complain to Grandmother. Little would she have cared how I felt.

Bitter fears accompanied my daily walks to the dreaded convent. Although my brother walked me there each morning, he was not allowed beyond the gate. Grandmother never walked there with me again, and that was just as well. I still shuddered at the pain of her grip and the sting of her rejection that first day. And now, the seemingly endless flight of stairs down to the school was a long, lonely journey. Everyday was torment.

Speaking very little French at first, I couldn't keep up with the school work. The result was daily punishment.

"Yaffa, read aloud the story of the cow," commanded the teacher-nun one day in French.

With all eyes on me, I merely gazed at my book, stupefied by fear and inability to read the French.

"*Allez, Allez!* (Hurry!)" she raised her voice impatiently, "We must go on with the lesson..."

I couldn't bear to give her the satisfaction of mocking my lack of knowledge in front of a class ready to laugh. Deliberately, I remained silent.

Grandmother spoke fluent French, so the nun assumed I did as well. Most of the story was etched in my memory, since the nun had already read it aloud. Were it not for my fear of the nun, I could have easily imitated her. I thought the story infantile anyway, with a title like, *"La Mu Mu"* (nickname for "the cow").

"You must speak out in class, little Jewish girl, or be

punished for disobedience!"

My fear of punishment was only a hair less intense than that of speaking out. Angered, I made up my mind that from that day on, no one would hear my voice, least of all the pasty-faced nuns. The vicious cycle began. For my "disobedience," they rapped the knuckles of my tiny hands with a ruler. For the pain they inflicted, and for the humiliation they caused, I never once yielded. Even when I later understood more French, no one was going to know it! Lest Grandmother add to my daily punishments, I dared not tell of them even to my brother, in whom I otherwise confided.

One cloudy morning, upon reaching the convent with my brother and our dog, Tomi, I begged Mischa to wait until I was out of sight. Halfway downstairs, I discovered there was no handkerchief in my pocket. I swung my head in panic toward Mischa who was frantically waving one shouting, "Grandmother put it in *my* pocket by mistake!" The consequences terrified me. It was strictly forbidden to come to this school without a handkerchief. I knew it was too late to run back upstairs, for I was being watched and awaited by a nun.

Deliberately slowing my pace, I continued down the stairs. Each step represented graver punishment to me while I made sure my eyes didn't meet the nun's eyes. She shook her head as much as she was able in her stiff head and neck covering, and addressed me as I descended the last step.

*"Mademoiselle* Yaffa," she gurgled in French, "don't look so scared. I saw your brother waving your handkerchief. No punishment will come to you this time, but let me warn you that I shall no longer consider a

handkerchief in someone else's possession to be yours. *Allez,* let us do what we must.''

''What we must,'' included the ritual of taking care of our toileting needs in one of the two outhouses that stood like an insult in the courtyard. There was to be no leaving the classrooms for such a reason later. The danger of falling into the holes of the outhouses required the nun's assistance. But even at age four, to be lined up and stripped of our underpants before the other girls was humiliating.

That done, we were to solemnly bow to the life-sized statue of *Marie,* which stood in the middle of this huge courtyard. Then we were to form a cross on our little bodies with our hand. All these I carelessly rushed through. I was not going to sincerely bow before a ''graven image.'' Then we were marched, single file, to the right of the statue, farther into the courtyard and into the classrooms. The school was set underground, and everywhere the air smelled stale.

*''Bonjour mes enfants,''* (Good morning my children) began the teacher-nun with formal, forced sweetness. We stood still the instant she entered.

*''Bonjour ma Mere,''* (Good morning my mother) we chorused, almost mockingly. After this we were permitted to sit on long benches attached to long desks. Three bench-tables stood side by side in each row, filling the length and width of the crowded classroom. The benches had an uncomfortable contoured back-slant that must have been designed for adults.

We were no sooner seated than we were ordered to turn around and kneel on these hard rounded benches to face the back wall. To a statue of a crucified man, we were to say a prayer in unison. His name I refused to pronounce, chalking up demerits toward punishment. *Father would have approved of my Jewish pride,* I told myself, while I kept slipping forward, hitting my bony knees against the back of the bench. I never found a reasonably comfortable spot, and when I slipped, I was thought to be squirming during prayer. For this also, punishment came.

During recesses, I stood aside, sadly watching my classmates at play.

"See that little Jewish midget over there?" The pointing finger of a tall girl made me feel like running home.

"I wonder if she can talk. I never see her open her mouth," mocked another girl.

*And I never will!* I promised myself.

This became a daily routine, with nearly the same dialogue between the same two girls, so much that I envisioned it every time I stepped out of the classroom. Nearly everyday I was provoked to tears, both on the playground by the children, and in class by the teacher. That is why, by age five, I considered the steps leading down to the "dungeon-school" my personal Hell.

# chapter two

# *Where is Yaffa?*

**Persecution for being Jewish** in a Jewish country was not at all exemplary or typical of Israeli life. Certainly, it was not an expected experience. But then, I was neither a typical Israeli, nor was I leading the typically Israeli life.

Though Father was still in the navy, we had moved into our first stone house which we shared with two other Hungarian Jewish families. One was a childless couple, the Hermans. They adored me but, because of Grandmother, they refrained from paying too much attention to me. When she caught me jabbering with them, Grandmother's frown ended the session. The other family had a girl about my age, named Lisa, who became my only friend. Good thing, for Grandmother was forever preoccupied, or talking with our live-in neighbors. Often she would have a nervous fit and without warning just haul off and hit me. I learned to stay out of her way when she was in a bad mood. Countless times I left the house and walked the streets. Certainly, there was plenty to keep me occupied there.

One diversion was a visit with a kind Arab woman up the street who spun wool for a living. Daily she let me watch her work in her stone-floored courtyard. Another usual excursion was to the "egg lady's" house. Like a puppy I followed her in and out as she loaded her horse-drawn cart. Arab merchants used horse or donkey-drawn carts, shouting as they peddled their merchandise throughout town.

On hot summer days, I often followed a cart laden with watermelons or prickly pears on ice. My mouth watered as I watched customers choose and sample melons, then carry them away.

When a cart was full of prickly pears, however, the peddler handled this unusual little fruit with gloves, a frighteningly huge, sharp knife and lightning speed. I gazed in amazement as he whacked off one end, then the other without slicing his hand. Next he slit the skin across the two ends and quickly pried it open for the customer to take out the red juicy fruit. Often the peddler paid dearly for handling this small but uncooperative fruit as the tiny spines would penetrate his thick gloves if he hesitated too long. Oh, how I longed to be in the customer's place, for prickly pears were my favorite fruit.

In Israel, a native Jew is called *Sabra* (prickly pear). The Israeli-born is likened to the distinctive characteristics of this cactus fruit: a prickly exterior but a tender heart. Israel's need for natives in these early years as a nation produced an unwritten law saying that any Jewish child who speaks his first words and takes his first steps in Israel is a native. I was considered a *Sabra*.

The title *Sabra* is carried with pride, almost as much

pride as the Jewish heritage. Living with daily reproach over divorced parents, our poverty, and my convent schooling, I gladly welcomed being considered a native. Mischa, who was six years my elder, did not get this privilege.

Mischa was suddenly getting busy with school and his own activities, causing me to see less of him. Being without him was difficult for me, for he was the only one older than myself to whom I could relate. Till now, Mischa had been playmate, brother, father, and mentor, all wrapped up in one, and I was used to going everywhere with him. Now I was beginning to be an embarrassing shadow in the presence of his male friends. After school, I was told to occupy myself.

Utterly exasperated with my life's circumstances, I resolved to escape. Returning home from the convent one day, I grasped the hand of my friend, commanding, "Come on Lisa, we're taking a long walk."

"We walk every day," she replied, somewhat surprised.

"This is different, because we're not coming back. I hate it here, and if you're my friend, you'll come."

Our street was but about eight blocks long, and the uphill slope ended with a high stone wall. A long walk was impossible. Daily we walked this short street, stopping often along the way. But today our walk was cut short by this wall, leaving us with only one choice.

Lisa was unaware of my plan to climb the wall. I hoped she'd make the first suggestion to do so. My hint should have made it easy for her, but Lisa did not catch my remark about the "long" walk.

"Where can we walk now? I am not allowed on any other street," she whined.

"No one ever said we couldn't climb the wall," I said, knowing well my statement was misleading. "Don't you wonder what's on the other side?" I tempted.

"I guess, but how?"

"We can do it, Lisa. I can climb trees real well. I learned it from my brother."

"I wish your brother were here to show us how to climb this wall."

*"I'll* show you," I said bravely, and apart from Lisa's cowardice and a scrape or two, we did well.

On the other side of the wall we found a rocky expanse with a few trees. We boldly marched across the field before realizing we were headed for another city. Little did we know that city was Tel-Aviv, the largest city in Israel. This wall marked the border between Yaffo and Tel-Aviv.

"I don't want to walk anymore. Can we stop? I'm scared," Lisa protested, looking around her nervously.

"Alright, let's sit down on these rocks for now," I agreed, making sure she didn't sense my own courage dwindling. As long as someone else was afraid, I could feign bravery.

Oblivious of time and the concern our absence was generating, we chatted and played to keep our spirits up. By sundown Lisa's stomach was growling almost as loudly as she was. "If you didn't want to go back home, why didn't you bring some food!"

"I couldn't. All we had was flour and that awful powdered milk. I know Grandmother planned to use them up for supper."

"Aren't you hungry?" she asked with a quiver in her voice. The evening chill was beginning to sting.

"No," I said flatly, "I'm just glad to be away from home, and not to have to go to school tomorrow."

By this time Grandmother had searched the surrounding city streets over and over, stopping everyone she met.

In her frustration, Grandmother yanked the arm of a man walking by her, shouting, "Yaffa, where is Yaffa?" She was nearly hysterical.

"Stop shouting, crazy lady, you are in Yaffo," replied the man, freeing his arm out of her clutches.

"No, no," Grandmother protested, pointing to the ground, "Not this Yaffa; *my* Yaffa!"

Unable to pronounce Hebrew words correctly, Grandmother's "Yaffa" with an "a" and "Yaffo" with an "o" sounded the same to those who heard her.

It didn't occur to her that such small girls could climb the stone wall, so in desperation she called the police who also searched in vain.

That night passed. Next day, questioning all the Arab neighbors in Yaffo, the police traced the several visits to merchants we had made in our neighborhood. Since these were our daily routine, no one had thought anything unusual of them. Now the police had no choice but to climb the wall themselves, for all of little Yaffo had been searched. There, the two policemen found us sound asleep, huddled against the wall.

"I have never seen such stupid inconsideration!" scolded Grandmother when we were finally brought home. "Do you realize what you've put me through? You are never to climb that wall again, understand?"

Speechless and frightened by the police intervention, I merely nodded in my usual way, for I was no longer dealing with my coward friend Lisa, but with authoritative, angry Grandmother. The punishment I received I felt was undeserved, considering my circumstances. Yet never speaking disrespectfully to my elders, I suppressed my agony. Next morning, forced to go to school, Grandmother threatened further punishment upon my return. She did this to assure that I wouldn't disappear after school. How tempting it was not to return home!

During the severe spanking upon my return from school, I was tearfully aware that the hands which were punishing me were responsible for the distress that prompted my escape.

Just as I first feared, more and more Arab children avoided and mocked me since I "joined the ghost-creatures." Except for Lisa's parents, who had to live in the same house with us, many Jewish parents in the community warned their children to stay away from me. Now I was not only an abominable product of divorce, but worse -- a "Christian." Regularly hearing backbiting remarks about me, the sting of rejection became as common to me as the sound of my name. Yet its commonness rendered it no less painful. This, too, I could express to no one. Unfair and unbearable as it seemed, I bore the pain alone.

# chapter three

# *Strange Friendship*

**It was moving day.** Our family was going to live in a larger city. Father was out of the navy and would take up his skills as an artist to try to make a living. In the beautiful port city of Haifa our new abode awaited -- another stone building. It was better than the one in Yaffo, but again situated in the Arab section of town. Once a British military office building, it was now divided into apartment-sized sections.

We now had two rooms to ourselves. One room served as family bedroom, and the other as everything else. Father and Mischa hung a curtain across about a third of the all-purpose room. Behind the curtain we placed our ice box, two kerosene burners on a table for cooking, and an old china cabinet. A small sink was installed opposite the ice

17

box. Two large, round enamel basins tucked under the table, one for washing dishes, the other for our sponge baths, completed our make-believe kitchen.

A bathroom we shared with the only other Jewish family in the three-story building. The rest were Arabs. At first this was difficult for us, as we had never lived with Arabs in the same structure before.

Moving day was a memorable experience. Arriving in the afternoon with our few belongings, we lined up in a row, each carrying an armload, to march single file through the massive door. Before we reached a flight of ten steps leading to our apartment, I became uncomfortably aware of being watched. Glancing to my left, I caught a glimpse of seven bald-headed Arab children of various sizes standing next to each other in a line. With piercing, angry eyes they were standing in a courtyard half a story below us. The rest of our family could scarcely miss such a warm welcome.

Wondering whether the bald children were boys, girls or a mixture, we all marched up our steps pretending to ignore the laughable, yet uncomfortable scene. Clearly, Arab silence clashed with Jewish silence. The air was so tense we tiptoed up to our apartment.

Inside the apartment I heard Grandmother's cynical remarks to Father, "They look at us like we were aliens from the moon, while they are the ones who could pass for characters out of a science fiction movie. I don't like them, Laszlo."

"Don't worry, Mother, neither do they like us."

By the time we carried the second load up the stairs from the borrowed flatbed, we heard what sounded like a heated argument. None of us was able to understand it, but the loudness seemed to be unpleasantly directed at us. On the way down again, we were surprised by two filthy, bleating sheep that seemed to have come out of their living quarters. A choking whiff of potent sheep odor sent us rushing down the steps, involuntarily holding our breath until we were in the fresh air.

"What do you suppose they're arguing about?" Grandmother asked Father as we sized up the last load.

"They probably want us to leave. After all, we *are* enemies. Could I paint a grotesque picture of these angry, bald Arabs! We must be careful, Mother, don't provoke them. You know how they can be. Look, now their mother is sitting on the floor of the courtyard, no doubt to protect her children."

Barely settled in our new abode, Grandmother, standing on our balcony which overlooked this Arab family's courtyard, shouted something in Hungarian, disregarding Father's warning. Immediately, the mother sprang to her chubby, calloused, near-black feet, loudly reciprocating with Arabic curse words. Hungarian and Arab darts flew back and forth. Mischa tried to create peace in Hebrew, but no one understood it. This bilingual squabble was a mysterious exchange of strong, hateful vibrations between the two women, and was fast becoming a spectacle to all the neighbors in the building. Arabs below us, above us, to our right, and some peering through the main door from the street surrounded us with noisy curiosity. Then they all joined in the shouting.

Self-conscious, and perhaps feeling outnumbered, Grandmother quietly withdrew into the apartment, unnoticed by the still arguing neighbors. Now they were left to stare at each other instead of at her. That ended the matter, and, for once, I thought she acted wisely. This episode became a family favorite, and for years to come we laughed as we reenacted Grandmother's clever disappearance.

The daily squabbles continued to break the monotony of our lives, especially when Grandmother continued to beat the throw rugs over the balcony rail, sending down clouds of dust. There were times when the Arab mother tried to stop Grandmother by extending both arms up toward her with palms in a begging position. I used to feel pity for her at those moments, as Grandmother merely mumbled in Hungarian, "There is nowhere else I can beat the rug. What does she expect me to do?"

One afternoon, I heard foreign, though vaguely familiar words spoken between Grandmother and the downstairs lady. I could tell the words were non-argumentative. Puzzled by this sudden change, I stepped onto the balcony to eavesdrop just as the two women finished with reasonably friendly greetings.

"What happened, Grandma?" I questioned in Hungarian, "What language were you speaking?"

"You should know, Yaffa," she snapped impatiently as we both entered our all-purpose room. "It was French," she gloated. "We found a common language."

My embarrassment prevented pursuing the inquiry. Yes, I should have listened to their words, but I was too preoccupied with their changed attitudes.

Total confusion took place -- something Babylon must have experienced when God confused its inhabitants' languages -- during attempted communication between the two families. Our family stood on our balcony; theirs in their courtyard. Only Grandmother and the downstairs lady spoke French. None of us knew Arabic. The Arab family, Grandmother, and Father spoke no Hebrew. How could we all attempt to participate in conversation without burdening the two women to translate everything into and from French? We managed, somehow, using ample amounts of sign and body language. Mischa and I compared similar words between Hebrew and Arabic.

Sometimes Grandmother forgot what language she was speaking, and rattled off a string of Hungarian words instead of French ones. Then the Arab lady wrinkled her nose, shook her head, and retreated out of sight.

Desire for the two families to become reasonably friendly forced Mischa and me to learn Arabic in a hurry. When the newness of their common language wore off, and when Mischa and I were able to express ourselves, Grandmother's eagerness turned sour. An occasional shouting dual still prevailed. Between the women, only a strained, cautious and suspicious relationship developed. Not so for Mischa and me.

Soon after our arrival, thick, kinky dark hair grew on those bald heads. By now we knew their names and that their heads had been shaved to rid them of lice.

The youngest child of this Arab family was near my age. Her name was Furial, (pronounced foor-yahl). Our friendship grew rapidly in spite of Grandmother's warning: "Never forget who *they* are downstairs. I am sure they always remember who *we* are, even when they seem to be friendly. Don't take foolish chances. They could stab you in the back."

"Don't worry, Grandma," I assured her, "I know Furial will never turn her back on me. She's my best friend."

"At your age there is no "best" friend; you'll forget about her in no time. You ought to play with your own kind," she retorted.

*My own kind? They avoid me like the plague lest I "convert" them. As far as I am concerned, Furial is my own kind.* I felt like crying until, unexpectedly, Father spoke.

"Mother, stop telling her whom to play with," he seemed to defend me, only I wasn't supposed to understand the German. "Were it not for the children's friendship with the Arabs, we'd be living in constant fear of them."

"But Laszlo, I don't believe they need to be quite so chummy with them. Every time they return from downstairs, I nearly vomit from the sheep and rabbit odors on their

22

clothes. I get chills just thinking about it.''

True to her inability to stop complaining after making her point, she went on. ''Some of those people's habits make me cringe, like every time I hear those stomach-churning shrills of a mouse or rat they set on fire in the small rabbit cage... then the smell! Or when the chubby Arab mother starts that ugly yodeling in Arabic, loud enough to cause an earthquake. Why do the Arab women need to do that when one of their children gets married? Can't they just have a civilized, quiet ceremony? I wonder which one of their children is next...''

''If you want her to have Jewish friends,'' Father ignored her hysterics, ''enroll her in Jewish public school, where every Jewish child should be. She is already nearly six. I thought at least you'd try to enroll her in a Jewish school when we moved from Yaffo. Why did you place her in a convent again?''

''Alright, Laszlo, for once you are right. At the end of the month, I'll take care of it.''

I disappeared from the scene to go downstairs to tell Furial the good news. No more religious double-standard.

''Furial, do you think God is Jewish, Moslem, or Catholic?'' I asked her. Furial was a Catholic Arab. The question was unfairly challenging her own loyalties. We sat in her cave-like playhouse, which had been cleared of sheep and rabbits, discussing religion in our childish way. Furial was torn between her faith and her heritage, yet never once denied that God could possibly be Jewish. With all my heart

23

I was hoping I was right.

It was at this point in my life that I developed the habit of whispering prayers to God, mimicking Father's occasional, inaudible whispers. At first the prayers were mere ritual, a way to console myself. Eventually, they became more meaningful.

While waiting for the month to pass, Furial and I decided to create a Hebrew-Arabic language. I suggested we use as many similar-sounding words from the two languages as we recognized. It worked remarkably well, for the most part, and in no time we were speaking the strangest language anyone around us had heard. It was our own secret language.

Since only I spoke both languages fluently, most words in our secret language were formed by me, but not without errors.

One clear afternoon, coming through the massive doorway hand-in-hand, ready to start playing, Furial suggested an activity in Arabic.

"Let's *erkod,* she said with excitement. (The word was not yet part of our new vocabulary.)

I agreed, misinterpreting its meaning for a similar-sounding Hebrew word.

Furial tugged, and I turned!

*"Erkod, erkod!* She shouted, pulling harder with each word.

"We need to start out slowly in one place."

"No, we need to go faster!"

"Slower. Maybe if I sing a song, you'll get the beat."

"Sing if you want Yaffa, but I'll go fast.

"I am doing what *you* wanted to do," I said, exasperated, then added, "Show me *your* way," and I let go of her hand.

"Like this," she took off running down the street, leaving me standing in surprise.

Upon hearing, *"erkod,"* Arabic for "run," my ear referred me to the Hebrew word *"lirkrod,"* meaning to dance.

Furial laughed all the way back up the sloped street, then grabbed my hand again, and we both went *erkod* Arabic style. My embarrassment and my usual seriousness prevented me from laughing. Instead, I thought of ways to improve our communication as we ran.

Sorting out my thoughts in different languages occupied much of my time. I never mixed or confused them. With the adults in my family, I could only speak Hungarian. Between Mischa and me, however, Hebrew became the sole way of communication. Even in the presence of any non-Hebrew speaking visitors, Mischa and I spoke Hebrew to each other, much to Father and Grandmother's aggravation.

Though I spoke Hungarian, as yet I could not read or write it. Each evening I would look forward to "reading" the Hungarian newspaper. With determination I studied the shapes of the various letters.

Sitting at Father's feet, looking up at the underside of his newspaper, I would ask, "Abba (Dad), what is this letter called; what sound does it make? Abba?... Can't you hear me?'' I would poke loudly. Father would then lose his place, scowl at me, turn the paper over and reluctantly answer my questions. I carefully committed each shape and sound to memory, not knowing how long my reluctant "tutor's" patience would last. Straightening out the paper and searching for the place where he left off, he would resume reading for a few minutes until the next time I poked at a letter and disturbed him.

For months I persisted. The more letters I recognized, the more often I would disturb Father's reading. My learning took place internally; I never vocalized it. Neither Grandmother nor Father were aware of the progress I was making, and reproved my unrelenting, distracting questions.

Undaunted, I resolved in my mind, *I'm going to prove to them soon that I can read and write, even if they won't help me!*

Little by little the letters and sounds made sense. Soon my questions pertained to words, then sentences, yet it never occurred to Father that I remembered anything. Writing followed a similar pattern with Father thinking I was merely trying to entertain myself. Soon I announced, ''I'm going to write a letter.''

''Don't be silly, five is too young to write a letter. You can't even read yet,'' discouraged Grandmother.

''Yes, I can! I'll show you,'' I beamed, grabbing a pencil and paper.

Grandmother and Father sat and watched in amazement

at the dining table as I composed a letter, unpolished, but nonetheless, a readable letter. Grandmother stood up and said to Father, "She's a born teacher, Laszlo."

That German was my eavesdropping language, Grandmother once rudely discovered when I inadvertently blurted out, "I know where you are going this evening, to a movie, not to your friend's house." Surprised, Grandmother saved face after she had lied about their plans. Despite this, she continued to use German with Father, believing I only understood isolated words. In communicating with our neighbors, Arabic became Mischa's and my fourth language.

More than once, our knowledge of Arabic proved helpful and even life-saving. Several times Mischa came home looking like he'd been beaten. He never told Father or Grandmother the truth so as not to alarm them, but he told me that some Arab youths had attacked him. Because he understood their plans to further gang up on him, he emerged victorious in successive attacks. Arab gang attacks were a common and feared occurrence in the slums.

Mischa became known among the Arab boys as unbeatable. Quick on his feet, though short for his age, he learned exactly how to counter their attacks. I was proud of his reputation and often had to use him as my protector.

Indeed, Grandmother's statement, "They could stab you in the back," was not far from the truth.

I would learn this some time later. One day, after an evening function at school, I was walking home on St. Luke

Street, where a black sign of a cross protruded sideways from the monastery wall. It was dark. A dim light shone on the white background of the sign from across the street. Then I saw a silvery flash, and it disappeared. I slowed down. A tall image of a person was barely perceptible, and the silvery flash was close to it. My heart was racing, but my feet froze. It was too late to take the long route home; I might be chased.

I decided to make a run for it, my only chance, I thought, to pass as quickly as possible. I forced my feet to comply, and before I knew it, was stopped in my tracks by an Arab young man who was standing by the monastery holding out his long arm, brandishing a knife. He smirked, reached in his pocket with his other hand and held out a handful of candy. When I didn't respond, he grabbed my hand and slapped the candy into it. He mumbled in Arabic something about someone betraying him and seemed to phase out of reality. I had to think with lightning speed, for the man looked unsafe.

Again, I opted to rely on the speed of my running. While his mind was preoccupied, I pretended to be undecided about the candy. Then, barely moving my arm I scattered the candies all over his feet. The instant he glanced at them, disappointed, I was gone. Fortunately, home was only two short blocks from there. All the way home, however, I expected that knife in my back. This was a fortunate escape. It was not usually this simple.

After this incident I was no longer allowed to walk home

by myself in the dark, and Mischa was appointed my guard. Strangely, neither Father nor Grandmother ever protected me this way. I should have been, at my age, watched more carefully. No one ever knew where I was, and while I walked mostly with Furial, it was to places no children should be.

*chapter four*

# Coffee, Bread and Paintings

**Our years in Haifa** were those of food rationing and hunger. The meager allowance of flour, grains, sugar, and coffee never lasted the month. For days at a time, our diet consisted of strong, syrupy German style coffee with milk. That was breakfast. For supper we broke chunks of bread into mugs, poured the syrupy coffee over it, and ate it like soup.

Our dog, Tomi, was not exempted. Hungrily, he lapped up coffee with bread chunks from his bowl. Even when we had other food, Grandmother fed him coffee. Her reasoning was that coffee would stunt his growth, hence make him a better indoor pet. Still, I thought it a strange diet for a dog.

I developed a distaste for the bitterness of the potent coffee and the smell of it brewing most all day. By the time I was twelve, I resolved never to taste coffee again, and to this day I have not.

Eating was not an important activity in my life. I did,

however, ask Grandmother one day, "How does it feel to be hungry?"

"Why, Yaffa, don't you know?" she answered, half surprised, half curious. "You are hungry when you feel a twinge of pain and emptiness in your stomach, and then you can't think of anything else but food."

Puzzled by her detailed description I sighed, "I guess I have never been hungry... and I don't want that pain, anyway."

Grandmother realized I wasn't being playful. Often I played a game when food was running low. I would ask, "What are you cooking, Grandmother?"

"Rock soup," she would retort, meaning, "Don't ask because it isn't adequate enough to mention." Though she was serious, I took it as a game, inventing more unlikely meals until I was told to stop.

This time the game did not continue, but rather, it marked the advent of uncomfortable medical research for years to come, to find the reason for my lack of hunger. I hated those tests. I felt like a laboratory mouse, having to swallow nauseating castor oil as a laxative, followed by hours of waiting, then drinking cupfuls of red-dyed chemicals and more waiting. Then I was off to the x-ray room. This process was repeated countless times in different hospitals throughout Israel. It was eventually concluded, several years later, that I had a shrunken stomach as a result of the lack of nourishment during infancy. This, they claimed, contributed to my lack of growth.

During this time when we were "rich," there were pancakes for dinner, and when we were truly "wealthy," my brother and I were sent to the Arab merchants with a large platter to fill with their famous *hummus* made of pureed garbanzos. We also brought home some flat, round pocket bread called *pita*. Then we each broke finger size pieces of the *pita* to dip in the *hummus* -- Arab style. Delicious! It was a family favorite.

Having eaten so little all my life it didn't take much to fill up. Often a mere two or three bites was my capacity. With something I truly enjoyed, like hummus, I managed a little more. It was such a welcome change from that bitter coffee.

The smell of coffee was not the only offense to my nostrils in those days. Since Father was an artist, our all-purpose room became part studio. I grew up with the acrid smell of oil paints as well. Always an unfinished painting stood on the easel. An occasional painting was commissioned, but that was the exception. Mostly we just hoped someone could afford to buy it.

Luxuries such as art work were out of place those years in Israel, making Father and his formerly highly esteemed skills nearly useless. Israel needed those who could work with pick and shovel, not pencil and brush. As a result, we drew upon every available source to make a little money, mostly creative projects.

For a regrettably short season we made greeting cards with beautiful dried flower arrangements on the front. For hours we walked, picking wild flowers. Then we squeezed the moisture from stems and petals and placed them flattened on separate pages of large books in varying positions for drying. A few weeks later the flowers were ready to glue in attractive combinations on the front of folded cards, and covered with a thin sheet of cellophane paper.

Father, Mischa, and I worked feverishly during the spring when field flowers were abundant. The hours of flower-picking were favorite times for me. Second to that was inventing unique arrangements on the cards. I felt privileged that Father trusted me at such a young age to share in the work. Through it all, I discovered my own artistic abilities. Father never instructed me or criticized my work.

At last, the end of the month arrived. Grandmother kept her promise to enroll me in a Jewish public school. The school office was a painful reminder of the one in Yaffo. I forced myself this time to behave older than I felt and I held my breath as the registrar opened her mouth.

"Her birth certificate, do you have it?"

"I certainly do!" Grandmother slapped it on the desk and warned, "If you also reject my granddaughter for her frail size, I will take her back to the Catholics! *They* didn't ask questions."

"No need to get upset, all needed information is on the birth certificate. We don't relish sending Jewish children into the clutches of the Christians. Please have her come to school tomorrow at eight o'clock."

Grandmother expected to leave me there the same day. It seemed the registrar purposely made her wait.

It was pure relief to attend public school with my own kind, as Grandmother would put it, where Hebrew, the language I loved most, was spoken, and where no harsh punishment was given. Though my schoolwork was excellent in public school, I stubbornly refused to speak in class or on the playground. Until the fourth grade, the teachers were forced to base my grades solely on my written work. I still had the second highest grades among forty.

Whenever my teacher asked me a question in class, I froze. It seemed I had heard similar words before as she reproved me one day in exasperation.

"You cannot go on being silent in class, Yaffa. Class participation is as important as other forms of learning. If you continue this stubbornness, I will be forced to consult with your family about this."

*She can't scare me into talking,* I thought. Grandmother can't even communicate with her. Besides, she wouldn't bother coming to school.

I was wrong! In the middle of a class session, a few days later, the classroom door was suddenly thrown open, shocking us all. There stood Grandmother, her fiery eyes searching for me. Without warning, she marched up to me, ignoring my teacher's frantic efforts to calm her down, and shouted, "Yaffa, look at your book and start reading aloud right now!" She expected instant response.

*I wish I were invisible.* Dead quiet, the entire class had stopped working to listen to her angry Hungarian. Though few understood the language, all understood the issue.

"Read!" she commanded even louder, "Read out loud!" Her voice was frighteningly authoritative. Her head shook with anger. I knew she meant every syllable.

Stupefied, I merely stared at her.

Waiting a few moments, her head still shaking with her habitual nervous anger, she spoke for the third time.

"I came to school to make you read aloud and resolve this foolish stubbornness once and for all. Now look at your book and start reading." She forced her last words through gritted teeth.

With no intention of reading, especially because of the

idiotic scene Grandmother was creating, I clamped my lips shut and began to cry, lamenting my injured ego.

Suddenly, again without warning or mercy, Grandmother slapped me across the face with all her strength. Then she looked around her, enraged, and marched out of the classroom. As I pulled myself back onto my seat, I realized that for the first time in my life, I had won a battle with her.

I never wanted to face this teacher or this class again. Hitherto they thought I was unable to speak and now felt betrayed after the many recess hours of concentrated effort to "teach" me to speak.

I relished the only pampering I ever received when individual classmates tried to "teach" me simple words.

"Say mama, Yaffa... please, say it for me. I'll be your friend and help protect you," one would say.

"Don't force her," another would shout, "she probably can't talk."

With persistent silence I tried their patience. I took advantage of the only times I wasn't mocked, though even at these "learning sessions" on the playground, some couldn't take my silence, saying, "Let her be, she'll never talk. I never heard her say anything. It's a waste of time, let's play instead."

Often one of the boys would give me a shove, saying, "She's so small, she can't even stay on her feet when I push her. One of my "teachers" would then try to "protect" me by chasing the boy away. Soon I began to run from the boy as I saw him coming. I was a fast runner, and most of the time succeeded in outrunning my pursuers, while my "teacher" cheered me on. When the chase was over my "lesson" resumed.

In order to keep their attention, I pretended to make a great effort, ''m-m.''

''Look! she's trying to say something! That's very good, Yaffa, try harder, like this, ma-a-ma-a.''

Slowly, deliberately, I continued the game, and at different times it was a different classmate's patience I tried, with each one ''teaching'' me another word. After a while it was a matter of competition, to see who could ''teach'' me or coax me into saying a new word. My ''teacher's'' excitement in my ''progress'' provided me with enough courage to speak the words in the first place. And having begun pronouncing the word, I realized I had to finish it, or lose further attention.

''Mahm... mamma,'' I blurted out. By this time a crowd surrounded me, and my ''teacher'' responsible for my new word then gently led me to the teacher to report the ''miracle.''

Commended for his or her efforts, the successful classmate was then appointed my keeper for a week, supposedly to further influence me and to protect me from other children who meant to mock or harm me.

But now, because of Grandmother's humiliating outburst, the fad of teaching-Yaffa-to-speak ended, and again I was the loner, ridiculed for my size, my silence, and my odd Grandmother's behavior.

Upon entering fourth grade, an unusually kind teacher with fascinating teaching style, drew response from me. Unexpectedly one day, I blurted out an answer to her question. During the hush of surprise that followed, self-consciousness overwhelmed me. In an instant I realized there was no return. The class had heard me speaking normally, and I could no longer hide behind total silence.

The breakthrough of speaking outside of home brought with it the reward of a few friends with whom I could associate. Yet I remained speechless in the presence of strange adults for years to come.

Each morning, as we Jewish children walked to school, we passed the Armenian Catholic monastery on St. Luke Street where the sign of a cross protruded from the stone wall. Ever since the incident with the knife there, the instant my eyes met the sign I would spit on the ground in ritual. I learned to do this from the superstitious Arab children. We all did it to free us from any harm this hated symbol might impose on us. If I had any prejudice, it was toward the Catholic symbols which represented the punishment and agony I experienced in the convent.

During this period of time, I was sent to see a social worker who was to look out for my emotional and physical well-being. One day, this social worker took me to a psychiatrist to find the reason for my "stubborn" silence and to help snap me out of it. The psychiatrist was so discouraged, getting no response from me after long, one-sided sessions, that he declared, "She will probably never speak freely outside of family; it will be a lifelong habit. Send her to some foster homes on regular, but temporary, intervals to get her out of her usual environment."

As a kind of therapy, I was sent to several homes for short periods of time. I knew the social worker used this method to help put better and more consistent food in my stomach, so I could grow, and, indeed, to take me out of my abusive environment which she and the psychiatrist felt were causing my silence. Judith Simon was her name. She was a German Jewess, kind and caring. I overheard her concerned remarks to the psychiatrist in German, though my sessions were in Hebrew. It never occurred to me that my family life was "abnormal" until these comments. I am sure the two of them had no inkling that I understood their discussions. *Sabra's* were not expected to know German, anyway.

My foster homes experience lasted about two years, and then ended. I never stayed anywhere longer than a week. With no improvement in my social behavior, Mrs. Simon could no longer justify the therapy. I was classified an ultra-introvert and given no hope of recovery.

Certainly I would have been much better off not knowing my diagnosis. Once again, my secret knowledge of German brought me unwanted information. Now I began to worry that something was wrong with me.

More than ever I spent time on the street. Furial and I would walk to places like railroad tracks, searching for empty cigarette boxes. Each box we found we ripped apart so that the front and back looked like a card. Furial got one side and I the other. With the many brands of cigarettes there were, we collected a large number of cards, and then traded them with neighborhood children. Furial was my go-between, for I would not trade directly.

Barefoot and still wearing ill-fitting clothes, more than once I returned home with a broken chunk of glass or rusty nail in my foot. Often I would walk alone, my mind filled with puzzling questions about life.

One day, walking some distance from home, I noticed two Jewish boys from my school throwing rocks at a puppy. The little helpless dog yelped as the stones hit his undernourished, quivering body. For some time I stood there in shock, guiltily watching, too afraid to speak out. The pain of my personal fear and loneliness turned pity into self-realization. Wasn't it *I* who was always leaning against a door that would not open to protect me?

I could bear it no longer! Suddenly, I mustered a timid question, "Is this your dog?"

"No," they answered. "It was pestering us."

With pretended confidence, I walked over to the sad puppy, picked him up and took him home. What a victory that was. The boys were left standing there, too surprised to say anything.

"I know how you feel, little dog," I comforted him. "I get hit for no reason, too."

Knowing well that we would not have enough food to keep another dog, and that Grandmother would not allow it to stay in the house, I left it inside the massive door by our steps, sheepishly stepped up to our door, and seeing everyone dining, just stood there, looking sad.

"What is wrong?" someone asked. Just what I was hoping would happen. With tears rolling down my face, I related what I saw, and how I bravely rescued this dog from certain death, and couldn't we just spare a little food -- I would even give up my portion.

I succeeded. Half my meager portion and a little more was allotted. The dog stayed with us for about six months. Then I was forced to walk with him several miles away, tie him to a tree, and leave him. I cried all the way home.

In the course of time, I managed to bring home turtles, injured birds, a chameleon, and a few more dogs. My sad, dramatized stories with each of these nearly always succeeded. But every animal eventually met its end.

# chapter five

# *First Discovery*

**Israel was celebrating.** The air was saturated with infectiously joyous singing. Masses of young and old gathered in major streets throughout the day, bursting into dance. Independence Day, Israel's seventh birthday, May 14, 1955, was the occasion. On a day like this one, all Israel comes alive. As for me, Independence Day celebration was the only time of the year I felt alive.

Evening had settled upon us, but the celebration was hardly over. Twilight merely encouraged most Israelis to tirelessly folk dance under the bright street lights. It created an inspiring atmosphere. No matter where one was in the city, celebration sounds reached the ear, and the reason reached the heart.

Dancing in the beams of the street lights was the highlight of the day, and I, looking forward to it, searched for the perfect moment to break into a dance circle. Inside some of these giant circles one or two inner circles were forming.

This was the time for the skilled, coordinated and brave to dance, of which there were countless. To watch these inner circles dancing the opposite direction from their outer circle was in itself a dizzying experience, but to participate was ecstasy. Considering myself an advanced dancer, I contemplated entering in. It took hours of watching for me to gain courage. Just then, I was rudely summoned to join Father and Grandmother who were walking on Allenby Street, unresponsive to the celebration. This meant I couldn't finish celebrating. My heart had already set my feet a-dancing, and my eyes could almost see the upcoming fireworks.

Disappointed, I stalled, knowing well the reason I had been called away. Father and Grandmother did not celebrate. They joined no one and nothing. Though they, too, were out walking, their destination was "work." Hardly caring that my favorite moments were just spoiled, their call persisted. From a distance, as if they couldn't bring themselves to approach the scene of celebration, Grandmother gestured for immediate response.

Reluctantly breaking away, I ran to meet them. The three of us headed for the senior club where Grandmother worked two or three hours each night. Usually we all pitched in to help, but since Mischa received permission to remain with the celebrants, I was required to perform my own duties as well as the various duties normally assigned to him. As beloved and trusted coordinator of this club, Grandmother was poorly paid. Yet she devoted much time and effort to provide activities. This day, the daily walk from home to the club took about half-an-hour.

Lusty singing, jingling tambourines and clapping dictated

the involuntary tempo of my steps. I hated the thought that all this would soon end and life return to its normal sadness and I did not get the chance to participate in the height of the celebration.

Eight years old, with seemingly millions of questions on my mind, I mulled over a few in particular for a long while before asking them. Always first carefully weighing the consequences before speaking, I rarely said more than I had planned to say. Fear held back any other words. I determined to ask some nagging questions I never before braved.

"Abba, how can I be eight years old when all of Israel is only seven?"

They laughed. I was insulted, thinking my well-considered question deserved a serious answer.

"You are... heh... older... heh, heh... because you were born before the rebirth of Israel," Father managed, trying to control his laughter.

"I still don't understand, Abba, how one little girl could be older than a country."

Again they laughed. Aggravated but not letting on, I asked another premeditated question.

"How did we come to live in Israel?"

"Oh Yaffa, that is a complicated story you don't need to know yet," came the almost expected, but disappointing reply from Father.

"But, Abba," I pleaded, "I must know because I am so confused now." Fragments of our story, which I had overheard and understood throughout the years when they commiserated in German, I already knew. These fragments were stashed away in my mind in a mass of confusion, and I was obsessed with the idea that I could somehow manipulate a conversation to complete the past in my mind.

"There is no stopping her now, I suppose," said Grandmother to Father in German. "She'll always wonder if we don't tell her something. Tell her, Laszlo, the parts she can cope with," she abdicated.

As usual, I merely pretended to be patiently waiting for my answer in Hungarian.

Carefully choosing his words, Father paused with each sentence for a sign of support or disapproval from his mother.

"You were born in 1946, after the war had ended," He began as if I didn't know. "We came to Israel, then called Palestine..."

*Came? He means "escaped."*

"You were not even a year old," he articulated, as if speaking to a five year old. "So you see, a country can be any age, and that age does not depend upon the age of its people."

I wasn't getting the answers I wanted, facts that would pull the fragments together, so I could understand my past, and myself.

"How old was Germany when we left there?" I asked abruptly.

Father quickly glanced at his mother, and both their facial expressions changed so drastically that I was sure I had said something I wasn't supposed to. Mentioning Germany seemed to have struck a sensitive cord.

"Laszlo, we can't keep it from her any longer," insisted Grandmother in German.

"I can't bear to tell her about it, Mother."

"We'll do it together, and by the time we get to the club

it will be over," promised Grandmother, yet she never told me anything. Now I felt responsible for the torment I saw in Father's face.

Sparked by Israel's birthday celebration, my questions triggered Grandmother's decision for Father to tell me a carefully calculated version of the truth. For over a year now, I had a longing to know about the past. The "fragments," though disturbing in nature, aroused my curiosity, and now I felt incomplete.

I wondered why the comparison between my age and Israel's age caused laughter, whereas my questioning the age of Germany triggered a complicated response. As we kept walking, Father's voice began to sound like a teacher of patriotism.

"Always be proud of being a Jewess," he lectured. "In Israel it is a privilege to be Jewish, but in Europe it meant persecution."

*I've heard this admonition before,* agonizing over the fact that while in the convent, no such pride in my heritage was possible.

"What's persecution?" I asked, though I knew well what it was. I pretended not to know, to assure the conversation continued.

"That's when one kind of people mistreats another because of racial, religious or political prejudice..."

"Just like what happened to me in the conv..." I choked off what I intended to emphasize. I committed a rare mistake, needing terribly to draw empathy from Father. He had no knowledge of the extent of my convent persecution. No one did. My comment seemed to have gone unnoticed. Father was too wrapped up in his own world of misery, as he always was.

Out of respect for him in his emotional state, I politely nodded every so often -- a European gesture -- to indicate that I was listening. I knew I mustn't unduly upset him. It was a rule in our home. Father tended to get depressed these days, then emotionally ill.

As we continued walking to the club, I suddenly realized that we were no longer marching to the happy tempo of Israeli folk songs.

In the absence of the celebration sounds, listening to Father's story was agony. He told of cruelties and unthinkable tortures. Carried away, much of what he said I deemed unfit for my eight year old ears. Grandmother never stopped him, and I wondered why. In about twenty minutes, the history of the Holocaust and its reasons boggled my mind. But it was impersonal. No details were supplied to piece my "fragments" together. I still felt disconnected, bonded with no one except with Mischa.

*Why was I abandoned as a young child?* I cried inside. *Didn't anyone love me?*

Now Grandmother spoke, but not to me. Her tone of voice was harsh. I almost expected her to say those very words, for they frequented her lips, often at inappropriate moments like these -- usually in German, but this time in Hungarian. She spoke as if I were not with them, one of her aggravating habits. Yet it was obvious she wanted to convey the information to me.

"If the children's mother were not so hard-headed, things could have turned out differently in Europe. Laszlo, I always knew she was no good for you. It's a pity she comes to visit the children. She fills their minds with untrue stories about me. Then it takes days to convince them she lied. All those gallant acts she claimed to perform in concentration and refugee camps, I did! She thinks she saved our lives, hah!"

"Mother, let's not talk about that now," protested Father, and then succumbed. "Ruth did plenty to help, but you hated her so... never gave her a chance to prove herself."

"Just the same, Laszlo," Grandmother raised her voice, "I think you ought to be firmer when she comes for them. Once every two months is too often, even if it was the court's decision. She is trying to buy their love, but it won't work."

"If only you'd let her in the house every once in a while, we could calmly explain things to her, and..."

"Never! That woman does not belong in our home. Just like I said, you ought to be firmer."

Though Father managed to tell me some facts, they managed to ruin my day. Forgetting my original questions, I was hoping Father would win the argument, but all our voices suddenly hushed. We approached the senior club.

Work went on as usual, but for me, this was not a usual day. Silently, I served tea and imported British biscuits to the glum card-playing seniors who were almost oblivious to our presence.

When the evening ended, I was glad. On our uneasy walk home, I thought over the peculiar answers to my "legitimate questions." My mind had been filled, but my emotions were left in turmoil. Instead of gaining, I felt I lost something.

*chapter six*

# God is Not a Mouse

**Our family religious background** was typical. Except for Grandmother, we were a generation of "modern" Jews, who, while claiming, "We were born Jews, and will die Jews," were blind to see that between birth and death we are utterly void.

People like our family had a vague respect for God, but not even a form of religiosity to show it. We did have a basic knowledge of the Old Testament, but nothing in it was ever mentioned. Father never said the blessing over our meager food, though at other times he prayed silently by himself. Such a practice would have been attractive to me, for I always had a tendency toward God. Anything to show trust in God would have comforted me in my confused state.

Yet, with a distorted view of what it means to be Jewish, we ate *matzo* on Passover as a substitute for leavened bread in the coffee. In our eyes, hatred for Christianity equalled pride in our Jewish heritage. Grandmother was the exception to the Jewish pride. To save her life, and perhaps her family, during the war she agreed to become war correspondent for the Nazis. Considered an abominable act, it was akin to renouncing Judaism and her own people. To my knowledge, she had always embraced an atheistic attitude. Father believed in God, yet he never took the religious lead. God was not mentioned in our home. My own instinctive interest in God drove me to question Him and reason with Him concerning the religious double-standards in my upbringing. I was desperately holding on to my Jewish identity, refusing to follow in Grandmother's footsteps.

The convent experience in my tender years caused my private hatred for Christianity. No matter what was forced upon me, my Jewish instincts prevailed. I detested "graven images," crosses, and pictures of "Mary," and the like. Mention the name of Jesus, and my entire being shook with angry hatred, and my stomach churned with disgust.

Nevertheless, my friendship with Furial persevered despite her Catholic upbringing. I ignored the detested "graven images" in her home. Her attitude toward Jews was unlike that of the other Arabs as well as of other "Christians." We had a sisterly bond that superseded what either of our families' religion dictated.

The Moslem religion, with its deep-seated hatred for the Jews (as well as Christians), seemed absurd to me and defied trust in God. Living in a predominantly Moslem Arabic community, the Moslem motto, "We will drive the Jews into the sea," was a familiar one.

In the center of Haifa's large Arab community, there was a minaret, a tall cylinder shaped tower, visible from all directions. At the top, a wrought iron rail enclosed a narrow circular balcony. From that circular balcony a Moslem crier called to worship all Moslems in the city five times a day.

His voice repeatedly pierced its way into the air with deafening decibels, *"Allah hoo akbar! Allah hoo akbar! Allah hoo akbar!..."*

Daybreak, morning, noon, mid-afternoon, sundown and late evening, this chant is the Moslem declaration of faith, "God is great." During the inescapable, high-pitched, throaty chanting, we Jews who lived in the Arab section of Haifa were prone to a headache. Indeed, everyone heard it, but few responded.

The last word in this statement *(akbar)* meaning "great," sounded nearly identical to the Hebrew word, "mouse." So as the Moslem priest screamed out, *"Allah hoo akbar,"* I tried to drown out the offensive noise with my fingers in my ears mocking, "God is a mouse! God is a mouse! God is a mouse!..." for however many times it was chanted. I was not alone in this mockery, but perhaps went to greater lengths to express it. While mocking these words with my mouth, I remembered the Moslem motto, "We will drive the Jews into the sea" and thought, *You can't drive the Jews into the sea, because your God is a mouse.*

But then, who was *my* God? Though I was unsure, I longed to trust in a God who was bigger than a Moslem "mouse," more real than Christian "graven images" and better than Jewish Passover chicken soup with *matzo* balls. I struggled to identify such a God, but had nowhere to search.

My past, with its mysterious gaps, was still a package of impersonal events to me, in which, as yet, I had not been mentioned. How I longed for someone to tell me about *me*! I felt as if I belonged to no one. Family ties were as loose as could be, and even those few who survived the war hated one another. I was disgusted with my relatives, and the rest of humanity, with their ruthless ways and prejudices, almost ashamed to be part of the human race.

This is why I found myself talking to God concerning the Arab-Israeli conflict. I longed for peace, not only nationally, but between individuals. Longing for peace is a prevalent Jewish emotion, dating back to Biblical times. We show it even as we greet one another with *Shalom* (peace).

Several times, lying upon my bed, I contemplated, telling God how I would like to visit the Egyptian Arab leader, then Nasser. Frankly but kindly, I would express my desire for peaceful coexistence. I would share with Nasser that Furial and I have been closest of friends for over six years. *If only their religion didn't dictate the annihilation of the Israelis, it would be possible to get along,* I thought.

That Furial and I were inseparable friends, and not even war between Arabs and Jews could pull us apart was proven one day during the war of 1956. Air raids screamed their way into our lives one morning when I was on the way to school. War rarely stopped normal activity in Israel. Everyone was well trained and drilled for emergencies.

This particular morning, military planes had been flying over Haifa and other cities for at least two days. As schoolchildren, we were taught to judge for ourselves, if caught in an air raid, whether we were closest to a bomb shelter at school or by our homes. Some public buildings and residential communities had underground shelters.

I remember, vividly, the precise moment and spot when the air raid siren invaded my peaceful walk. It was about two blocks from home. I was fortunate not to be caught midway to school where no shelter was available. Just as the deafening air raid siren blasted, I turned around toward home catching sight of Furial on her way to her Arabic school on another street. I screamed and motioned for her to join me. Without hesitation she ran to meet me. Then the two of us grabbed each other by the arm and ran full speed toward the Jewish shelter. It was already filling up with Israelis. We hurried in, Furial still attached to me, and I was in no way going to let her go. Furial and I sat huddled close together, despite the raised Jewish eyebrows and puzzled stares. Their eyes scolded me as if to say, *"To play with Arabs on the street is one thing, but to cling to one in a Jewish bomb shelter when we are at war with them is another!"* I didn't budge.

After this event I told God that I wanted to become an ambassador when I grew up, and to use my experiences with prejudice to offer solutions. My lofty aspirations were distracted and later forgotten with Grandmother's sudden illness. Absentminded, nervous, and often unfair or abusive, she was all I had for a "mother."

Though sick and helpless, Israeli hospitals refused to keep her, believing she had typhoid. We were ordered to burn all her belongings to prevent a plague. Later, it was discovered that she had stomach cancer. But by that time she had wasted away to skin and bone.

As the only other female in the family, it was my responsibility, at age eleven, to care for Grandmother. She could no longer walk, so several times daily I would help her to the bathroom and back to bed. I had received special permission from school to remain at home and do my schoolwork there. Between my schoolwork, nursing "job" and helping to keep the house clean, I had no time for play.

Worst of all my chores was giving Grandmother daily sponge baths in the round, enamel basin behind the curtains. The offensive odor of her cancerous body nauseated me. With tears obstructing my vision, I bathed her each day for eight months. Though her body was thin and languid, her weight was still heavy for me to support. No one ever offered to help me get her from bed to basin. I was merely expected to fill the roll of nurse. To that was added the role of housekeeper. Because of the demand upon my time during those eight months, I hardly saw the outdoors.

Life was full of apprehension those days, as we knew Grandmother would soon die. The cancer had by now consumed her stomach and was viciously spreading toward her heart. Unable to eat, she sipped only water and broth from a teaspoon. Our activities centered around Grandmother's needs and often undecipherable demands. During the day, if I hadn't noticed her demands, I was told to leave my schoolwork to answer her call. It usually involved spooning water into Grandmother's parched mouth. It was a twenty-four hour task. Father took over the night shift.

With Grandmother's every squirm and whimper, my heart jumped. I agonized with her in silent strain, holding my breath, as if to help her feeble efforts to speak out. The experience was wearing at me. Getting much too little sleep, my schoolwork suffered. I was in dire need of a break.

We suspected that the major deciding factor why the hospitals and doctors sent Grandmother home in her condition was our obvious poverty. With no cooperation from our socialized, but as yet disorganized medical system, we desperately turned to a British missionary doctor. He agreed to come to our aid. Daily, he came to check on her, and then pumped her bloated stomach of cancerous fluid. By the day, her condition was worsening.

This missionary doctor was our first and only contact with a Protestant Christian. Were it not for our desperation, we would have never turned to him. For Father, it was a most difficult and troubling decision.

In exchange for the missionary's services, Father painted a replica of a famous British painting. It was a horse and carriage in a country setting. How beautiful I thought it was! Father's remarkable skill and workmanship made it indistinguishable from the original. He used a photograph of it which the doctor had taken before coming to Israel. The original painting hung in an English museum. Father, I am sure, shed many a secret tear over that work of art, realizing that more than likely when it was finished, his mother would be also.

Aunt Marga, Father's sister, was with us at last, to relieve me. She moved Grandmother's bed to the all purpose room. One evening, all four of us were nervously awaiting the doctor's verdict in the bedroom. The examination and treatment took longer than usual. Slowly, the doctor lifted three fingers to us. This meant that Grandmother might live three more days at the most. Sad, yet relieved, all agreed she had suffered enough.

Despite her cancer-infested heart, Grandmother had a

determined will to live, managing to survive three weeks longer than expected. One of her last rational statements was a command, "Take that dirty comb off the dining table, haven't I taught you never to do that?" Grandmother may have been harsh and difficult, but she always kept our humble, poorly furnished abode clean. For weeks after her death we marveled at that statement.

It was on the last day of her life that Father decided to send me to a friend's home, to spare me the agony of witnessing Grandmother's death. She was by then nearly unrecognizable, completely irrational, crying out desperately to us for sips of water with languishing whimpers. I was no longer in charge of her care, and often her requests were ignored.

I felt a guilty relief as Father led me to the door, with her laying there so helpless. One more last look, and out we went, silent and sad, leaving behind us Aunt Marga, my brother, and a strange, sickening mixed odor of oil paint, coffee and cancer.

*chapter seven*

# Bat Mitzvah

**Morning brought the expected message** that Grandmother had died. I forced myself to shed no tears, remaining aloof and quiet for the few days during my stay with our friends. Though the family tried to cheer me up, I did not respond.

Upon my return home, Father was sitting on a low stool sadly staring at the floor. In Jewish tradition, the closest male related to the deceased sits in prayerful mourning for seven days, as many hours each day as he can possibly bear. The entire mourning period lasts thirty days during which time no celebration is tolerated. Father spoke to no one during this tense period. I returned to school, but could not apply myself.

Soon after the thirty-day mourning period, I turned twelve. That meant a *bat mitzvah* -- the advent of semi-adulthood. Religious families conduct a special ceremony in the synagogue, especially for a boy. Non-practicing Jews merely put on an extra special party. We could not afford such a party, nor could we bear to celebrate yet.

How painfully empty it was in our kitchen area without Grandmother! Our attempts to cook our meals failed so miserably that we were forced to spend the last of our funds on platters of Arab *hummus* and *pita* (the lazy way out). Our lives became disoriented, but we carried on the best we could.

"Yaffa, the ladies at the senior club decided to organize and pay for your *bat mitzvah* party," Father spoke to me for the first time since the day before Grandmother died. "They insisted, in memory of Grandmother," he continued, obviously holding back his distress. "It will take place at the club."

"What? How can I celebrate so soon? Don't they take *my* feelings into consideration? I can't bear to go into that club," I answered, feeling both guilty for my ungratefulness, and hurt for the lack of tactfulness on the part of the club members. I knew that without the club I could never have a proper *bat mitzvah*. Yet I wanted to reject the opportunity, never to celebrate as long as I lived.

Father was already painting for them a portrait of Grandmother from a photograph. They insisted even after Father's refusal. It was the worst likeness I had ever seen Father paint. He rushed it. They wanted to hang it on the wall at the club. What a cruel, inappropriate request! If they had only known the tears shed over that painting and how hard it was for him to work on it so soon. But they didn't think of that, just as they didn't think of what a party at the club might do to me. I wished to be left out of their selfish attempts to show their sorrow. They should have shown

58

their appreciation of her while she was alive. Instead they took everything she did for the club for granted, constantly complaining. And though she was president, she did all the manual labor that no one else wanted to do. I know, because I helped nearly every day, clearing the dirty tables, washing them off, setting them for the next day's activities, cleaning the kitchen and bathrooms -- all the menial work. No club member ever lifted a finger. Father was more aware of this than I. It must have aggravated him.

"No, that's not fair," I protested, "I don't want to go there, ever. It reminds me of everything. I can't pretend."

"You must go... already invited guests... made arrangements."

Father started speaking in fragmented sentences, so typical of him when he is under too much stress. That was the key to our recognizing his instability. It frightened me. Wanting to spare him further distress, I reconsidered.

"All right, I'll go, Abba, but only for Grandmother." I lied, but I couldn't tell him it was really for him.

He nodded with a contemplative unemotional smile, another "sign." He had no more to say on the subject.

*My poor Abba,* I thought. *Here I am, being selfish about a stupid birthday party, while he is attempting to care for us alone and falling apart.*

*I must watch out for Father,* I determined. I was the only one who knew he had already been on the verge of a breakdown during Grandmother's last week of life. No one had time or patience to watch his behavior. Aunt Marga, when she was with us, and Mischa were always busy discussing plans for after the inevitable. I, however, had my eyes and ears open to anything that could distress him. It came instinctively, ever since the trauma of his first serious emotional breakdown when I was eight. That experience rendered me afraid to be alone with Father, though I respected him.

During that time his behavior frightened me so much that I begged Mischa to take me out of the house. It was three in the morning. Mischa was left in charge as Grandmother hurried to get a doctor. Father was stalking the kitchen, breaking things. I was trembling with fright, and as much as I loved Father, I did not want to be around him. After much entreating and tears, Mischa realized I was terror-struck, and complied. We walked up and down our street, never veering too far, in case Grandmother came back. Before she returned with a doctor, I was further frightened by a policeman's rude questioning.

"What are you two children doing on the street at this hour!" he ordered.

"Our father is emotionally ill, and we cannot be with him until a doctor comes with medicine to calm him down," cleverly replied Mischa. The policeman let us go.

I was overwhelmed with embarrassment. Never had I heard the words "emotionally ill," but I sensed their seriousness. My embarrassment, however, didn't measure up to the terror I felt inside the apartment. When we saw the doctor leave, Mischa and I returned.

Now four years later, convinced that Father was close to another attack, I thought I should alert Mischa before the *bat mitzvah*. I did, and Mischa contacted the doctor. He was told to watch for other symptoms and report back. With me going to school and Mischa out looking for work, the task was nearly impossible. At sixteen, Mischa decided to work by day and school by evening. He was seldom home.

Meanwhile, my entire class of forty, and two or three teachers were present at my *bat mitzvah* party. It was, to me, a mock-celebration. The very last thing I needed or wanted to hear at this occasion and in this place was a speech about Grandmother's noble character in relation to the club. I didn't recognize most of those qualities in her at home. The speech sounded like a cheap eulogy, embellished to the point of absurdity. Exaggerated and melodramatic, it was completely out of place at a birthday party. *Is this necessary?* I agonized.

Painfully, impatiently, I endured the long one-hour speech, shedding my first tears since the shock of Grandmother's death, and wishing I had never been born myself. The many gifts I received and unwrapped toward the end of the party meant nothing to me. I was too numb to care, although in my entire life I had never been so lavished with presents.

Choking while songs were being sung in my honor by my classmates, I was unable to control the flow of tears. Beautiful and touching melodies were selected from the Songs of Solomon, some of my favorite folk songs. Their words alone triggered emotion.

At last it was over. With no goodbyes or thanks, I walked out toward home, alone and empty-handed, purposely leaving guests, hosts, and gifts behind. *Let them have it all!* screamed my heart.

*chapter eight*

# *What Now God?*

**Mischa awoke unusually early** the morning after my pathetic *bat mitzvah* party. He was eager to be on his way to his first day as apprentice in a dental lab. I heard him preparing to leave and flew out of bed, dressed for school as quickly as possible, and darted out the door with him.

*Stay out of Father's way,* I told myself on the way to the balcony and into the chill of the pre-dawn darkness. Father's behavior had become more and more eery and I was afraid to be alone with him. So as not to ruin Mischa's triumph of at last finding a job, I restrained from expressing my strong feeling that Father was "on the verge." Mischa leapt onto every other of the ten steps and out the creaky, massive door onto the street. Shivering at the top of the cold, stone steps, I sat waiting for time to leave for school. Staring into the street through the open door, I wondered, *How did I become my father's keeper? With all the changes in their lives, Mischa looking for work, and Aunt Marga getting married and moving from Beer Sheba to Haifa, who else is left?*

Suddenly, the lights turned on in the all-purpose room. Peeking in the window that faced the balcony, I watched Father nearing the dining table. He had been feverishly working to finish a painting of Michelangelo's famous statue of Moses holding the stone tablets of the Ten Commandments. For once, the work was commissioned. I remember admiring the indistinguishable likeness to the photograph.

Painting Grandmother's portrait delayed the completion of this one, making a public official who prepaid Father angry.

Father was unaware that I was looking in. He was putting the finishing touches on the canvas. Abruptly, he disappeared behind the kitchen curtain, and returned with a long butcher knife. In horror, I watched him slash the large painting with a long X, mumbling something I couldn't hear.

I was unable to contact Mischa, and had no knowledge of where to find the doctor. Too frightened to stay, I started off to school, half dazed, half guilty. I remember making a mental comment about the ugly black cross as my eyes met it on the street. Instantly, I spit on the ground before passing it. Somehow, my superstitious fear of being "hurt" by this sign was intense that morning.

Oblivious of time, I walked slowly, wondering whether my circumstances would ever improve. As I continued walking and questioning, I felt myself fading away, lost in thought, until the piercing screams of...

"Watch out! Move away from the middle of the street!

Lady, will you grab her, please, and take her across? I've been honking my horn at her, but she didn't even budge.''

I heard these sounds, but I couldn't respond. Then I felt a forceful jerk on my arm that snapped me out of my sense of non-existence. The shocks I had been experiencing had finally registered in my mind, and I could bear them no more.

Before I could pull myself together, I was in front of my school principal being severely scolded for standing in the middle of the road. I remember feeling much younger than my age, not wanting the responsibility of knowing what I had gone through lately, and dreading Father's inevitable mental collapse.

On the way to my classroom I forced myself to "feel" mature -- a *bat mitzvah'd* girl just doesn't act like this. *According to the law I am now responsible for my actions, before God and before man,* I told myself as I walked into the classroom, pretending nothing had happened.

Just as I managed to convince myself that I was not insane, I was surprised by a circle of classmates next to the chalkboard. Being a lot shorter than they, I couldn't tell what the commotion was about, except that my presence created tension.

One of the girls, Sarah, came out of the circle, grabbed my hand and led me to the center of the crowd. Another girl -- the blabbermouth of the class -- blurted out, "See what Sarah wrote on the board?'' I turned around just as someone rushed to erase some Hebrew printing. Like a bullet, it penetrated my heart: "YAFFA'S GRANDMOTHER IS DEAD!''

"No! Don't do that to her, you made her cry.'' Sarah

pushed the blabbermouth away and put her arms around me as if to protect me, saying, "I didn't mean for you to see it. I just wanted to remind the others what happened to you so they will leave you alone. After watching you at your *bat mitzvah,* I decided to warn the class before you came. You looked so sad and helpless at your own party, it made me cry for you. Please believe me, it was supposed to be erased before you got in."

It was too late; the damage was done, and I tactfully wriggled my way out of Sarah's arms; no one had the right to touch me! Nothing registered during school. I couldn't read. I didn't understand what I heard.

Still carrying a mental picture of those large printed words on the board, on the way home I promised myself not to mention the incidents of this day. Father had enough of his own pain to carry... I was approaching the dreaded cross when, in a flash, my mental picture was forced to change.

"What's that ambulance doing in front of our house?" I whispered under my breath. I sped up out of curiosity, neglecting to spit on the ground before passing the black cross. That didn't matter right now -- nothing mattered. *"God! Why is Marga and Mischa next to that ambulance... don't let it be... please!"* I now ran at full speed to the scene with my heart pounding faster than my feet could run.

There it was, a large, white van with a red star of David. The entire downstairs Arab family was watching. The mother was shedding tears for whomever was about to be carried into the van. I could tell everyone knew that I had arrived, but no one said anything, and in my frantic fear, I couldn't find the words to ask.

Watching the downstairs lady's tears of tender concern, I

was amazed, for never had I seen her cry before. With the ambulance doors open, agonizing moments of silence passed. Then a man in white appeared upstairs at our door, holding one side of a cot. I knew it was Father, but, nevertheless, looked around me, hoping I would see him standing somewhere. Yes, it was Father. His dark hair was showing now. He was asleep, but why? Then, I remembered. Four years ago, they sedated him so they wouldn't have to convince him to cooperate. It seemed so cruel and selfish. Something one would do to an animal. *Why didn't I try harder to do something when I saw it coming this morning?*

The Arab lady sorrowfully wiped her tears as she watched the cot being carried down the stairs, out the massive door, and into the ambulance. She was standing directly across from me. Still no one spoke. I needed so much to have someone -- anyone -- say something comforting to me. I looked toward the Arab lady, then to Mischa, standing close to her. No one noticed me or my need. Instead, Aunt Marga climbed into the ambulance, shaking her head ''no'' at Mischa's attempt to follow her in. He was to stay with me. The ambulance doors shut and quickly, without the siren, took off, leaving us in the midst of a crowd of curious, speechless bystanders.

Now I ran to Mischa, but could not manage to talk. The words just refused to come. Too much was on my heart -- too many mental pictures for one day. My mind was weary, my emotions overburdened. This day brought nothing but grief to me. *No one would believe me if I did manage to find the words to tell about it.* In spite of Mischa's presence, I felt forlorn, wondering what life was going to hit me with next. What would Mischa and I do on our own?

As we headed for the apartment, someone sadly commented, "The doctor said this time its for life." My heart sank, knowing where Father was being taken. *What now, God?* I thought, not even able to whisper to Him.

That horrible day of three emotionally draining incidents left me void of ambition and I completely neglected my schoolwork. Spending much time daydreaming instead, I imagined Grandmother yelling at me, Father painting at his easel, and Mischa and me speaking Hebrew in spite of Grandmother's complaints. I desperately wanted to bring it all back, though I knew such a scene was gone forever.

Not even two weeks passed before my make-believe world was cruelly shattered. "No! Not you Mischa! They can't take *you* away! What will I do alone?" I wailed when Mischa's draft notice arrived.

"Don't worry, Yaffa," Mischa said flatly before he left. "Marga is going to see that you are cared for." Even Mischa's voice was void of feeling.

Marga? In my dream-world I didn't even acknowledge her occasional presence with us. Although I loved her, I had no room for her in my emotional chaos. As far as I was concerned, I was now alone with our starving dog. Poor Tomi, an injury some years before left him with only three legs. He was now confused, sad, like me. Seeing his ribs protruding from hunger, even I in my calamities felt pity for him. He was faithful through all our ordeals, which is more than I felt I could say for my family at this time. *They all left me. But perhaps Aunt Marga will stay by me...*

While immersed in these thoughts, I heard commotion outside. I poked my head through the window, overlooking the street.

"No! Wait! Please don't take my dog away from me too!" I screeched, as the city pound coldly threw him into a closed truck. I bolted out the door and ran after the truck with all my strength. Tomi was going to be put to sleep, for he had been roaming the streets, searching for Grandmother, his master for all his seven years.

I ran senselessly, chasing the truck as far as my legs would carry me. Defeated, I watched in helpless agony the animal truck disappear without mercy.

My mind again flashed back to the ordeal of Father being taken away in the ambulance only two and-a-half weeks before. I sobbed unashamedly, in the middle of the street, not for Tomi or for Father, but for myself, shuddering at the prospect of being completely alone. *Abandoned again...*

*chapter nine*

# Orphanage

**Officially, I became** property -- or so it felt -- of the welfare society. With Aunt Marga's consent, they decided to place me in a communal orphanage. *Not even Marga,* I thought, *was standing by me. For Father, she chose the institution, for Tomi, to be put away. Why me also? Did she have to choose to place me somewhere, like unwanted animals or sick people?*

Aunt Marga refused to even let me stay over-night during the week of orphanage arrangements. She had me sleeping at home, half way across town, and coming to their apartment after school for supper. I never did appreciate this, for I was so alone and afraid in the empty apartment. Sad, angry and eery memories, recent and past, were my unwelcome companions.

My walks to their home were filled with a strange, mixed feeling of loving my aunt but hating her decisions. *She didn't even try to keep me in the family,* I bemoaned, *but just handed me over to the state.* How the feeling of rejection stung! I felt cheated, and given no chance to cling to the only relative who remained capable of caring for me. "God, why is she doing this to me?" I whispered on the way to Aunt Marga's on my last afternoon of city life.

I barely cared where I was being taken. Purposely, I numbed myself to keep from feeling the sting of Aunt Marga's desertion. To prevent thinking about it, during the forty-minute train ride I tried to lose myself in past experiences... Grandmother singing German and Hungarian songs... perhaps the only happy moments I had around her.

Hard as I tried, I was unable to dwell on this scene for long. My mind diverted me to the more recent incident of my mother's latest allotted visit. With all that happened in the few months since, I had forgotten about her and her outrageous request.

I now remembered Grandmother warning us on her death bed, "Your mother will try to lure you to America."

Thinking back to that argumentative visit with my mother, I recalled Mischa's flat refusal in spite of Grandmother's imminent death. Faithful little sister that I was, I agreed with him shouting, "That's right, I never want to be with you."

*No doubt she married the American tourist to help her get to the "land of the rich,"* I now thought in silent mockery. *Who wants America, anyway!*

As the train screeched to a grinding halt, reluctantly, I came back to the present. We found ourselves in a scenic country area between Haifa and Tel-Aviv. From the train station we walked about a mile, and the gates that would keep me enclosed with two hundred other children became visible. I wondered if this place would echo a Jewish version of my convent experiences.

I wouldn't touch the closed gates when we approached them, impolitely letting Aunt Marga usher me through and onto a dirt road that seemingly went nowhere. Seeing no sign of life, she wondered if we were lost. *Good! I don't care if we are lost,* I thought, *since Aunt Marga is throwing me into this orphanage just like Tomi was thrown into the truck.*

Aunt Marga's close contact and cooperation with the welfare society had given me a feeling that no one knew what to do with me. I should have seen that desertion was next. Never had I been truly at home anywhere. And now, could I call this strange place a home? *God,* I prayed silently as we noticed an office sign. *I would much rather be with Furial's family.* Then a stab of regret went through me as I realized that I hadn't even said goodbye to her. *Will I ever see her again?*

In the office, Aunt Marga filled out some forms, doing her best to converse in broken Hebrew. Then she found a counselor, said a hurried, awkward goodbye and went on her way.

As soon as Aunt Marga left, the children of my age group were scheduled for a field trip. It was a hike up the beautiful hills of the town of *Natania.*

"Good timing," I heard someone say, and I was off. *Good timing indeed!* Hiking was one of my favorite pastimes and, having just walked a mile, my legs were primed. It was an unusually warm day for February and after obvious rainfall, the ground smelled invitingly fresh. I had never experienced such open air, and decided to make the best of it.

Vast rows of golden yellow wheat swayed rhythmically in the cool breeze. Sun rays hung between small clusters of fluffy white clouds as they marched across the clear blue sky. I was sure this was going to be my best hike yet.

Usually a top rate hiker (a frequently practiced sport in school), I reached destinations at the front of my group. This day, I lagged farther and farther behind. Soon I became warm. Then I became hot and weak.

The journey upon a counselor's shoulder to the small but attractive hospital in the orphanage, I did not remember. This was a nurse's station with hospital-like accommodations where doctors from nearby cities made weekly visits to treat the serious cases. They would come more often during emergencies. I was one of those emergencies, I was told. I had passed out.

At first I was thought to have an ordinary cold with a fever. As the days went on, my cold turned to measles. In isolation, the nurses watched over me day and night, for my undernourished, frail body was not showing signs of improvement. A simple case of the measles became a threat to my life.

Children in a communal may, at high school age, choose a trade or profession, receiving on-the-job training there. One of the nurses who took care of me was such a trainee, about seventeen years old. Her name was Varda. Although an orphan, she displayed unusual love and compassion.

Adopting me as her "little sister," Varda visited several times a day, doing everything she could to cheer me up. Even during my quarantine days, she peeked in several times daily to see how I was doing physically as well as emotionally. Eventually allowed to enter my room, Varda spent much time at my bedside, asking questions and listening to me. Her kind of love and attention is what I had longed for all my childhood. She was a *Sabra,* mature and self-assured.

In the darkened room with the smell of disinfectant and medicine, I had nothing else to do but to introspect. With all my heart, I wanted to reach out in some way to thank Varda for her friendship. *Why can't I? I hate my timid self!*

"Yaffa'le, all I see when I look at you is a pair of large, sad eyes, and a tiny body," Varda would say endearingly. Though she was looking for even a hint of a smile, I could never bring myself to it.

For weeks I lay in bed dejected. Hearing happy sounds of healthy children at play, I at least wanted to see them. The blinds were drawn to prevent damage to my eyes, and to no avail I begged the nurses to open them. It seemed I was never to leave the little hospital.

A month passed before the long-awaited day finally arrived. After dressing, I was allowed to leave my bed for the first time. Looking out the back door of my room, I welcomed the sunshine and the cheerful sounds of chirping birds. Three days later I was, at last, dismissed.

Because of my immediate illness on my day of arrival, I had never seen my assigned dormitory room. For the first time, I met my house mother who gave me a tour of all the dormitories.

"Here is your new home," she pointed as we stopped by the second door of one of the long buildings. Little did she know what the words "new home" did to me. Nervously standing in the doorway, I caught a glimpse of four beds, each next to a wall. "You can go in and make your bed," she pointed to a bare mattress on a rusty coiled spring. Hesitantly, I entered. A wooden orange crate turned on its side with one shelf and a little curtain at its opening stood at the foot of each bed for our meager belongings. The other three girls were at school. I hadn't even met them. It was just as well I saw the room alone. One new thing at a time was enough.

One of the first rules I was told about by our house mother concerned the upkeep of our room. "You must turn your mattress over each morning before remaking your bed to allow it to wear evenly," she admonished. I listened carefully, fully intending to follow the instruction.

In our room, this much-disliked chore had long been turned into a morning wake-up exercise. To the count of three, they vaulted out of bed, hastily dressed, and then held a noisy race to see who could turn her mattress over the most times before collapsing. Disregarding which side was supposed to face upward that day, the girls merely worked up an appetite. The first morning, I was shocked at the noise and blatant disobedience, all the while expecting harsh punishment to follow. It never came. Soon, I dared to participate, if only halfheartedly.

Called a *mosad,* the communal orphanage was an institution accommodating children only, although run similarly to the *kibbutz* which includes entire families.

Three categories of children lived in my orphanage: true orphans, children from broken homes, such as I was, and a large percentage of European refugees. These Jewish refugee children came from Communist-controlled countries like Rumania, Poland, Czechoslovakia, and Hungary. They had been given up by their parents, some of whom were imprisoned, others restricted in activity or under strict guard. There was no guarantee that the parents would ever see their children again, since these countries would not let the parents emigrate. Hoping to give them a freer life, the parents sent or smuggled them to Israel. The Israeli government felt responsible for these children's welfare and education, and since the children had no relatives here, the orphanage was the only solution.

Of my three roommates, two spoke Hungarian, but not fluently. The other girl spoke Polish as her mother tongue. Only two of us spoke Hebrew well.

The Polish girl, a resourceful eleven-year-old, was one of those refugees that came alone to Israel. One of the Hungarian-speaking girls, Miriam, also spoke Italian, her mother tongue. Her Hungarian parents escaped to Italy before the war. When she turned twelve, they sent her to Israel to stay at the orphanage until they could manage to join her. She spoke very little Hebrew, and was also a newcomer.

My third roommate's name was also Miriam. She was a typical, native Israeli. As a *Sabra,* she was the kind of girl we all wished to be -- cocky, forward, brave and smart -- the prickly pear in person. For the first time it occurred to me how untypical of a "prickly pear" I was. We had nothing in common save two languages. *Her kind of personality could have been mine,* I thought, *but I am so emotionally wrung out... so disillusioned with life and people!*

Miriam's parents were Hungarian but she had spoken mostly Hebrew all her life. After her mother had died, she came to the orphanage upon her father's request. She had been here since infancy. We were quite a mixture. None of us were close friends, though we shared a common need.

With no interest in even trying, my school work at the orphanage was extremely poor. I had turned from a studious girl into a lazy thinker. During classes, daydreaming and flashbacks from recent months and years precluded any accomplishment. My low grades became an embarrassing concern to the school board, who couldn't understand why on the one hand I neglected my own studies, and on the other, helped the younger girls in my dorm with their homework. Becoming their personal tutor satisfied my need to be looked up to instead of mocked, although I was at least a head or two smaller than they.

Month after month, I managed to pass the time my way, mostly walking. I was embittered, not knowing whom to blame for my fate. Yet I was better off now than ever before, getting three good meals a day, a decent bed to sleep in, and most of all, no harsh punishment.

My sadness increased when Varda, my make-believe sister, was drafted to serve as nurse in the Israeli military. All Israeli girls were required to serve in the armed forces.

I missed Mischa and my Arab friend Furial. Here I was surrounded by Jewish people only. The atmosphere was drastically different from that of my first twelve years of city life, and I was trying to accept it.

My lonely walks became more frequent as I braved breaking the rules about leaving the premises. I didn't relish breaking rules, but my emotions, my mind, and my whole being were all laden with burdens I could not otherwise unload. Tragedies of my life echoed loudly within, and I found no escape from their sting. Without the walks, I couldn't cope, so I began skipping classes.

Nevertheless, it was a good life, aside from the adjustments and my loneliness. My loneliness was often eased in Bible class, my favorite school subject. This was a class I never skipped. Throughout public school in the city, the history of our people was taught from the Bible. The Old Testament was our textbook, as nothing else was available in the pioneering years. Here in the orphanage, my seventh grade Bible teacher often turned boring historical accounts into inspiring, memorable events. Under her teaching, I began to treasure my Biblical Jewish heritage, and one day a fresh view of God dawned upon me.

It happened while listening, entranced, to my teacher's account of the lives of Moses, David, and Elijah. She based their respective, unique relationships with God on their recorded prayers. The lesson seemed tailored to my own curiosity about God. As she read some of the prayers and related them to their individual kind of relationship with God, she got carried away and, consequently, so did I...

Her voice faded into the background. My mind kicked into high gear with questions screaming within me. *Why do we not pray as our forefathers did? Why can't I?*

With my heart still listening, my mind whisked me back into days of old, and I was now with Moses. Together with him, I heard God's voice from the burning bush. In holy reverence, I, too, took off my sandals. Then I wept with Moses before God when he was distressed over the stubbornness of our people.

Now I heard the prayers of King David, the most respected of all Hebrew kings. Together with him I rejoiced over God's mighty victories, bursting with silent song. Then, I was with Elijah. Along with him, I boldly proclaimed before the prophets of Baal our loyalty to the living God. I was so intensely involved in the events and the prayers of these three men of God that I cast myself not as one of the many Hebrew spectators of the times, but as a kindred heart alongside my forefathers. I felt as if I had the task of proving God to the people -- of reawakening desire to know Him.

The sound of the bell rudely ended the lesson. Most of the students noisily rushed out of this last class of the day. As for me, a different kind of lesson had just begun. With it came a quest to really know God. Until now, I thought only old people -- bent-over, bearded, wise Jews -- resembling Abraham, could have such a relationship with God.

After this challenging Bible class, I needed time to think. Off I went to the tomato field, unburdened to God, and reasoned with Him, *"King David was young when he prayed. What's wrong with me doing it, God? Everyone says that today we can't have a relationship like he had. Then why should we pray at all?"* My disapproval of repetitious, unspontaneous prayer now became apparent to me. But who was I to question the Jewish, Moslem and Christian established methods with God?

It was past the dinner hour. I had spent all afternoon thinking and talking to God. Quickly, I filled up on tomatoes even though they were against the rules to pick. Then, before I was missed and someone would be searching for me, I headed back to the dorm.

*chapter ten*

# Yaffa the Storyteller

**"Yaffa, Yaffa!"** came a voice rushing toward me when I returned from the tomato field. "Where have you been all afternoon?" quizzed a girl. I ignored her question. "We're having a contest. We need your help."

*Who would want my help?* I thought.

"What kind of contest?" I asked, as another girl approached with notebook and pencil.

"Our dorm and the boys' dorm, a story-writing contest, and we think you'll win."

So I had, after all, gained some kind of respect. I had no idea my bedtime stories had created such an impression on my roommates.

Since age eight, I had taken to writing short stories and poems. In fact, the thick notebooks filled with Hebrew writings were virtually my only possession upon entering the orphanage. Occasionally, I reread their pages, just to pass the time. Caught doing so one evening before bedtime, my roommates coaxed me into sharing some of the stories.

Ironically, in my favorite story, the main characters were an orphan girl and her older brother who lived in a tree house, and later found a family who adopted them. I had subconsciously, since age eight or nine imagined myself an orphan. Certainly on an emotional level, I was.

It was this orphan story that made a hit with my roommates. For weeks, nearly every night, lying in bed in the dark we comforted one another with the ending of this story. It consoled our hearts and fulfilled the dreams of our orphan mentalities. None of us having any person who could comfort us, the orphan story served its purpose. From then on, story-reading became a ritual in our room. Yet, we never associated one with another except at bedtime, and secretly, I was afraid of them.

Now they expected me to write the best story in a contest that included about fifty boys and girls. Within one week, we were to turn in our masterpieces. This was a compulsory project.

Somehow, confidence in my own ability drained when I thought of forty-nine others. My mind blanked out as though I had never had a creative thought. Each afternoon, children sprawled all over the porches and corridors thinking and writing; they all seemed full of wisdom, all but me. When it came to competition, I was too nervous and timid to be creative.

Four days later, with the pages of my notebook still blank, I wanted to back out. My roommates had nearly finished their stories, but they insisted mine was our only chance for victory, considering some of the girls in our dorm were poor in the Hebrew language.

Last day of the contest. Today we were to turn in our stories. All week I had been feeling guilty for not having written anything. At the same time I had a need to maintain the respect of my roommates. I knew that if I didn't write, I would lose the chance to find out whether they were right. Besides, they would never speak to me again. This they already implied in no uncertain terms. At this point I could not afford to lose the admiration of those I feared. Forcing myself to think, a title came to my mind, "The Magic Sewing Machine," and I began to create a story to go with it. The main character was a poor, old rejected widow, whose broken-down sewing machine suddenly became capable of sewing the king's garments.

Sitting on the porch in the sunshine, I made up for lost time and, finally, my pencil flew across the pages. Once the resources of my imagination were tapped, a river of thoughts came gushing out. What I had been given a week to do, was accomplished within about an hour. I had no choice, it was time to hand in the stories to our counselors. The winner was to be announced the next day during an outdoor picnic.

I was on edge, unable to concentrate on the meal at the picnic. There was teasing and arguing, betting and challenging, especially between boys and girls. I stayed to myself.

Silent, nervous and lost in thought, I was jarred out of them by some vaguely familiar words. Returning to reality, I was shocked to hear my story being read by one of the counselors. I was sure everyone heard my heart beating, and saw my face blushing. No one knew this was my story. I just thought I gave it away by my reaction. All were anxious to hear the author's name at the end. The boys protested, the girls cheered.

A huge bar of American chocolate was my prize. After the picnic, I snuck away and laid a small square of chocolate on each bed in the five rooms of our dorm. I wanted to show my appreciation for their trust in me, and lacking the courage to express it with words, I merely distributed my prize.

Back in the business of story-writing, as a result of the contest, I was challenged to share what I wrote by being nicknamed "Yaffa the Storyteller." Despite this privilege, the stories had to be pried out of me, and I never shared them unless I was sure the interest was sincere.

Many more writings were added to my thick pile of notebooks, which later travelled across the ocean to America. Eventually, I translated some of them and wrote others in the English language.

A year and a half passed in the orphanage. Various chores there taught me a little of everything. In a communal, all work is divided, the amount and kind of work depending on age. I had worked in the kitchen drying and stacking dishes, and picked vegetables from the vines of vast fields to prepare them for cooking. In the laundry, my chore was to fold and file away in the storage room the giant loads of uniforms as they came out of huge roller irons. These plain khaki uniforms I placed according to size in the appropriate cubicles that covered the walls. Now and then I fed the chickens in the large chicken house, planted various vegetables and trees, and even picked cotton by the sackful in the scorching summer sun. The experience was good for me, always making me feel that I had accomplished important tasks. I used to pretend that my work was needed and appreciated, though no one ever indicated that it was. I had an insatiable need to be needed, and would invent the appreciation in my mind.

Planting our own little vegetable gardens in allotted small squares of soil was a favorite project. We were encouraged to till and do with them as we pleased. Some of us developed beautiful little gardens. In public school we had a similar program. Agriculture was a required subject throughout elementary school in all Israel. There was a difference, however, between the agricultural programs of the city school and that of the orphanage. Here we had more freedom to make our own choices, and mistakes in judgment or skill were less detrimental. This I appreciated, for I never excelled in land-tilling, though I enjoyed growing the vegetables. With agriculture I managed to scathe by -- not so with my academics.

The orphanage school board became increasingly disturbed over my refusal to study. When they found that I wrote stories and poetry, I was called into the principal's office for the second time and given the ultimatum to pull up my grades.

I didn't comply, so the time came to leave the orphanage where I was but beginning to feel at home. In the meantime, I had been receiving letters from my mother, urging me to join her. She had by now been in America for nearly two years.

"I am fighting for your custody," she wrote. "If you agree to come, the law will grant it to me."

Knowing that Aunt Marga had been doing the same here in Israel, I wished to stay out of the fight between them. My mother and Aunt Marga had, since the divorce, not been on speaking terms. This is a frequent, ugly European practice that has puzzled me most of my life. More stubborn than children, family members and friends decide to become lifetime strangers as a result of some disagreement. Though I was the child, I was always ashamed of their behavior.

Aunt Marga was childless, having been widowed in World War II, shortly after her first marriage. Now she was no longer able to bear children. I was told by the school board that she had decided to take me in. I also had the choice to join my mother. Aunt Marga would certainly be my choice, rather than an estranged mother of whom I wanted no part.

So once again, I was to change homes. I consoled myself with memories of Aunt Marga. In those days, and during the years before, she meant more to me than my mother. Grandmother's death intensified my need for her affection. I thought perhaps it might be enjoyable to stay with her, especially since a psychiatrist advised a full year of rest from school. It was decided that my emotions had undergone excessive stress. I needed to be free of the pressures of school. *No school!*

Departure day arrived and with it a tinge of sadness upon leaving my *mosad*. I would miss the beauty of the oak forest in which it was located. On my many lonely walks, with its treasure hunts, I found turtles, birds, lizards, butterflies and colorful wild flowers. I also would miss the Friday evening folk dance parties. There, I found myself losing some of my willful solitude. Scenes of two hundred children cozied up in their blankets on the enormous lawn on summer evenings, watching American movies, projected onto a white sheet hung from the roof of a building, would remain etched in my memory. Most of all, I would miss hearing my roommates coaxing, "Yaffa, please read us the orphan story," and feeling glad that I obliged.

There were no tears, no goodbyes when I left. I merely grabbed my few belongings from my orange crate, and departed. The train station was a half hour's walk, in the little town of Natania. On the train I felt that I had gone through this very process more than once before, but wouldn't bring myself to remember when. Nothing was going to ruin the enjoyment of this train ride. Hill after hill, field after field were naturally carpeted with colorful wild flowers of all kinds. Then came the orange groves with rows and rows of green trees in blossom. The sight of them forced me to take a deep breath, as if to smell them, despite the closed windows.

*I might come back some day, to visit there, just to see if everything is the same.* I had to admit to myself that I actually liked it there. How could I have taken it so lightly? Even the abundant food in the orphanage was cooked by Hungarian chefs. I also had to accept that this had been the best year and a half of my life, though I was bitter about going there in the beginning.

In my mind, I was forgiving Aunt Marga for "placing" me in the *mosad* instead of taking me in. And now, headed for her house, I was overjoyed that she changed her mind. She and Uncle Gustav, even with all his aggravating quirks and dislike of children, could be my parents. For once, I could enjoy a family life.

*chapter eleven*

# Shall We Forsake Our Country?

**It wasn't a big city** where Aunt Marga now lived, but a new community situated atop a range of hills, with a panoramic view. Her tiny apartment was one of about a dozen duplexes side by side in an uneven row. One could see this long row of houses from the bottom of the hill in the neighboring city. From there they looked like they were on stilts. The name of our miniature town meant "Eagle Heights," whereas the town at the bottom was "Eagle."

Life in Eagle Heights was not what I'd expected. Most of the one year free of school I spent washing my clothes by hand, hanging them on the line, cleaning up the apartment, which included scrubbing the floor, and usually preparing some boiled potatoes by the time Aunt Marga and Uncle Gustav returned from work. This left me little time for play. Saturday afternoons, my only free afternoons, I usually spent hiking alone in the hills of Eagle Heights, picking wild flowers.

Bored and unhappy, I now wished I could attend school. After some time, however, I was befriended by an Eastern Jewish girl from Lebanon who spoke Arabic and poor Hebrew. I wasn't allowed outside the house until after supper, and then only for a short time. Mazal was unavailable to play then, so she knocked on my door each morning on her way to school. By then my aunt and uncle had left for work. At times her knocks became my alarm clock, for I would still be asleep on the couch. Other mornings I saw her through the window and would jump off the couch, grabbing my bedding as if for laundry, embarrassed. I slept in the front room instead of in the unused, spare bedroom. Why, I never understood.

Mazal and I then secretly spent about ten minutes planning our Saturday afternoon. Many times I would spend those precious ten minutes with her helping to finish her composition and grammar homework, of which she had a poor grasp. Her parents, speaking only Arabic, could not help her. Soon, I became known as the block's "homework helper" and personal tutor.

The community of Eagle Heights was comprised of foreign immigrants, some of whom spoke little or no Hebrew. The state of Israel provided these homes as it now attempted to do for all Jewish immigrants. Back in our pioneering years, no such housing was yet available.

An elderly couple who spoke no Hebrew and needed tutoring lived about four duplexes down the block. Though only thirteen, I was trusted to teach them Hebrew two evenings a week, communicating in Hungarian. For this job, which I took very seriously, I was well paid. Now at least my mind was occupied.

One day, my friend Mazal brought to me another girl, who was from Rumania, and was also in need of help with schoolwork. The ethnic contrast between the two Jewish girls -- one eastern, one western -- was so striking, it inspired me to write a play. The three of us became the cast. The girls were enthusiastic and willing, but were disappointing actresses. Several weeks of evening and Saturday coaching passed before I was satisfied. I then designed and sewed costumes, enlisting their help. That done, we planned to put up a sheet somewhere for a curtain and... well, we could invite the adults in the block for an audience.

Most of the adults in our block never got to see our play. After all the props had been finished, Mazal announced that our debut would take place at her school instead. She had convinced her teacher to arrange for her class to stay one afternoon after school to watch the play. She needed special credit projects to improve her near-failing grades. The play was her perfect solution. Though I wrote, directed and planned it, she received the credit. I didn't mind.

The play went remarkably well, and our songs at the end, after the curtain was closed, topped it off. Although we were a success, Aunt Marga did not seem to care. She saw the practices, yet she didn't bother to attend, or say anything to encourage me. I thought she would be pleased that I was doing something creative with others. Oh, how I longed for her approval! *Would that I were back at the orphanage.*

Toward the end of the full year of rest from school, I met

my brother in downtown Haifa, and accompanied him to the dental laboratory where he continued to apprentice having been discharged from the army. I heard that my mother had an attorney write from the United States and managed to have him discharged six months early for some "special circumstances." The reason for my journey to his work place was to get help in straightening my crooked teeth. Mischa was allowed to do this independently in his free time. Self-consciousness over my crooked teeth was partly responsible for my never smiling; feeling I had nothing to smile about was the other reason.

This morning, Mischa and I were to rendezvous at a downtown, Haifa bus station. He was already anxiously waiting for me when I arrived. A twenty-minute walk up hilly streets allowed us time for serious discussion, as we hadn't seen each other for several weeks. Mischa had only been out of the service for two months, trying desperately to make a living. At age twenty, he had already had six years of experience behind him in dental technology, but was getting too meager a salary, usually delinquent. I could tell something was on his mind. He wasn't joking around as he usually did.

With not an inkling as to what he was hinting at, I listened to him complain, "You know *Abba* will never be able to support us or care for us. This means being forced to be on welfare. Frankly, Yaffa, I am tired of it all, the struggles, the embarrassment, everything."

The degree of his seriousness frightened me. This subject matter was not the kind he would unburden on me. Mischa was *my* mentor, not I, his. His use of "us" in terms of support was puzzling, for he needed no support from Father at his age, and I was being cared for by Aunt Marga, I thought. Something was up.

"So what's the answer?" I asked apprehensively. He always had one.

"*Imma* (Mother) has been writing to me about going to America," he admitted.

My heart sank. "Yes, she wrote me also," I said flatly.

"I know we never wanted to be with her, but America is the land of opportunity... I am going to take advantage of it."

I was shocked. "But... but... Mischa, what about me? Do you expect me to be all by myself here while you're on the other side of the world?" I wailed.

These were the most unexpected words I had ever heard from my beloved brother. *How could he change his mind so suddenly? Did he forget our hatred of our mother... and discount what we had told her?*

Unable to bear the thought of life without him, I made a split-second decision against my convictions.

"All right, if you're going, I'm going too. Who knows, maybe we can still experience a family life." I knew I was playing right into his hand, but felt I had no choice.

"Good," he declared, as if he got the precise response he expected. "Now to tell Aunt Marga that you're leaving..."

"You... you will come and h-help me break the news to her, won't you." I stammered, nearly in tears.

"Of course I will. Stay with me until after work and I'll take the bus with you. Don't worry." We had at this point arrived at the lab.

Waiting for the end of Mischa's workday, I was dizzy with apprehension, afraid to break the news to my aunt, and was concerned whether I had made the right decision. I also worried about life in a strange country with a mother who was nearly a stranger, and her husband whom I had not met.

Riding home on the bus, I reprimanded myself for conceding so quickly. I could have at least given it a little time and perhaps come up with an alternative. Mischa was uncomfortable and untypically quiet. As we descended the bus atop Eagle Heights' hill, I feigned a happy attitude.

"Shalom Marga!" I managed.

"Where have you been all day? You were supposed to be home hours ago!" she scolded, ignoring Mischa.

*So she is already angry.* With Mischa right behind me, I had hoped she would take it well. Mischa remained silent, forcing me to brave telling the news.

"Marga, I...," I started slowly, and then in the fastest Hungarian I could speak, it gushed out with pretended excitement. "I've decided to go to America with Mischa, isn't that wonderful?"

Slap! I reeled under the hardest blow she had ever given me, barely hearing her angry protest.

"Wonderful?" she mocked, "You mean selfish, Yaffa. Don't you realize that tomorrow is the day I was going to sign the final papers for custody? Nearly a year of legal fighting with your mother, and you just decide to go..."

No, I *hadn't* been aware *tomorrow* was that triumphant day for my aunt. Mischa must have known, for she always told him everything. He probably couldn't bring himself to approach Aunt Marga for me, since he was close to her, much closer than I could ever hope to be.

It was over now. There was nothing Aunt Marga could do if I wanted to go, and it looked like I was siding with my mother. Aunt Marga neither knew, nor could she have understood the true reason for my decision.

In a few days, pulling herself together, Aunt Marga became helpful -- almost too helpful -- in getting our emigration affairs arranged. Medical checkups, immunizations, drawing up of passports and purchasing all the articles needed for such a long trip lasted three months.

Out of necessity, Aunt Marga wrote a letter to my mother. Before sending it, she decided to read it to me. The letter had an air of coldness, like that of her knowing she lost the battle, and will never again be in touch. In it were details of my emotional problems as diagnosed by the psychiatrist, as well as her own opinion about me. In addition, there was a copy of a letter from the orphanage stating that my refusal to study coupled with my lack of physical growth were the reasons I was dismissed.

I was shocked and humiliated by her bluntness. *Who is my mother that she should be told of such personal things?* At first I could not understand why Aunt Marga read this to me. I realized that a small part of the letter was necessary, though it could have been more tactful. That she wished for me to know the details was the most painful part. Until custody was to be established, Aunt Marga was receiving a monthly sum of money from the government. That, too, she stated in the letter, implying that the sum was insufficient, and that I would ''cost'' my mother as I had ''cost'' her. Through these and similar statements I was beginning to feel that *I* was not the cause for Aunt Marga's fight for custody. There was family principle involved: Her ex-sister-in-law must not get custody. Now she could not bare to have lost to her rival.

In no uncertain terms, the letter was an account of "Yaffa the imperfect." When Aunt Marga read it to me, her attitude spoke as loudly as the words on the pages, *"Go ahead! Take her, she is unwanted here."* This was a more painful slap than the physical one. Finally, I understood, nearly too late... *Mischa did me a favor!*

That night, as I lay upon the brown-green tweed couch that had been my bed for nearly a year, I turned my head toward the empty spare bedroom, longingly. *Even if I had decided to stay, would I have ever really become part of this family?*

"God," I sighed in the darkness, "I'm going so far away this time. Perhaps I did make the right decision. At least Mischa hasn't deserted me."

*So what if we forsake our country,* I rationalized.

*chapter twelve*

# No Turning Back

*I would be living a lie,* I thought. *She's a stranger.* It bothered me that my mother thought she had victory. She thought I decided, after all my angry refusals, to live with her. *Could I bear to live with the one who abandoned me as a small child?* I dreaded the thought.

Everything felt ambiguous and surreal. Was this a bad dream? So many unfulfilled hopes I am leaving behind; so many unanswered questions lay before me. It was definitely too late now to change my mind, though the thought occurred to me. Already boarding the bus at Eagle Heights, we were on our way to Haifa's seaport.

The bus noisily whirled around the bend of Eagle Heights' hill. I jerked my head back for a last look at the uneven row of little houses. Today they reminded me of crooked teeth on toothpicks. *Never again will I see them,* I sighed. Now the bus had completed the turn, racing dangerously downhill, as if to deliberately take me away forever. In an instant the houses were no longer visible. *I must look straight ahead from now on,* I thought, and forced myself not to regret my decision to leave.

In an attempt to be brave and mature, I shut off my emotions for the remaining ride. Aunt Marga and even her husband accompanied Mischa and me on the bus. In my state of oblivion, I didn't even acknowledge their presence until Aunt Marga warned me, "Abba is going to meet us at the port. He's been allowed to leave the institution to say goodbye."

*Poor Father!* was my first deliberate thought since leaving Eagle Heights. *Are we deserting him?*

Nervously, I searched for Father from the window as the bus pulled into the port. There he was, sitting on a bench waiting for us, so alone. I could see his sad, drawn face. Once off the bus, I sat beside him to exchange farewells. I hadn't seen Father since he was carried off in the ambulance, except during his only visit at the orphanage nearly two years ago. That was an equally awkward visit. We barely spoke.

I was unsure of his mental and emotional state, and felt uneasy. Besides, with all that was on my mind concerning the big change ahead, I was too numb to initiate a conversation. I merely sat there, angry with myself for not even considering Father when I decided to leave. *Never mind that now,* I told myself. *It's too late for regrets.*

Motionless, speechless, I sat there waiting in agony. After several awkward moments, Father began speaking quietly, unemotionally, as if trying to remember a formal speech prepared ahead of time. With obvious effort to be brave, he stressed each syllable in each word with unnatural pauses.

"I hate to see both my children go to another part of the world where I may never see them again. For a father to part with his children when he has no one else, and is unfairly confined to an institution, is not easy. I sincerely hope your mother does all she can to make your new life easy. It was through no fault of mine that the welfare society took from me the custody of you, and now your mother succeeded in gaining it. Perhaps... perhaps it was meant to be that way. I want you to know, before you leave me forever with no one to trust, that I never intended to forsake you."

Still silent, I couldn't bear to look at him. He was preoccupied with his brand of misery, and I, with mine. Whether he or I needed consoling the most, I wasn't sure, but since he was the father and I the child, I had hoped he possessed the grace to reach out first. Then I thought I was speaking to him, but I wasn't. I merely spoke internally, as in a prayer. I heard it -- the emotional volume was unavoidable for me. *Abba, dear Abba, as much as I try, my mouth refuses to speak the words I am thinking. My heart refuses to reveal what I am feeling, though I love you and would not hurt you for the world! Please get well.* Suddenly, I was overwhelmed by the sting of the estrangement created between us since his last nervous breakdown. *How much I want to embrace you, Abba, but cannot! It just won't come.* Father was oblivious to my outcry.

Now that we were about to board the ship, I wondered if he understood anything that was in my heart and how I felt about him. Then, perhaps he wondered the same about me, for it was obvious I was to read between the lines of his farewell message.

Aunt Marga motioned that time was up. Both Father and I felt the urgency of the situation, and the pressure of time. Through obvious tears of self-pity he quickly mumbled, "You know, I'll die alone, and there will be no one to bury me."

*How does a daughter say goodbye to her father under these circumstances?* His last words were so desperate that I felt my heart couldn't carry the burden of their implication.

"I don't know what to say to that, Abba," I finally opened my mouth, my voice cracking from holding back the tears. "Let Marga help you. Don't be angry at her... Shalom."

Hopping off the bench to let Mischa sit next to Father for the remaining moments, I wondered sadly, *will it be as hard for Mischa as it was for me?* I could not bear to watch them. All I overheard was Father's complaint about Aunt Marga forcing him to stay in the institution, and Mischa's challenge, "Then prove yourself capable of making a living." I thought that cruel, but knew it was wise advice.

We made our way up the gangplank, Mischa and I, and boarded the majestic ship, *Zion*. It was by far the largest ship I had ever seen. I felt the size of an ant among the crowd that gathered at the rail. They were all waving and throwing kisses. Mischa proudly flashed a few pictures to remember our relatives by with his American camera, and we floated away, ever so slowly.

Frantically waving their hands, people on the dock gradually diminished in size, as if being shrunk. I caught a glimpse of Father standing among them, waving reluctantly. He looked sadder than anyone around him. I waved back, wishing I had hugged him. *My poor Abba,* I shed a tear, as I watched him turn into a speck among many specks of various colors. I continued to watch the specks blend into a blur while the edge of the cement dock blended into a horizontal line. I felt as if this line marked the end of my existence on the other side of it.

On board ship I felt a strange excitement mixed with confusion -- adventurous, yet sad. With all my determination I blocked out the past, pretending this was the beginning of my life. Not caring where I came from, or where I was headed, I numbly roamed the ship. With false curiosity, I checked out its every corner. All that mattered to me now was right before me, and I forced myself to concentrate on leaving the past behind -- to bring none of it with me.

# chapter thirteen

# *America, Here We Come!*

**Mischa and I** had adjacent cabins on the lower deck, not first class by any means. With three sets of bunks in each room, this was our temporary home for two weeks. We loved it. Towering three stories high, the beautiful white ship provided many exciting adventures for me. Climbing up and down the stairs, visiting different compartments and sections, some of which were out of bounds for passengers, I took advantage of having no obligations, no tasks or chores. For now I was captain -- the captain of this ship and of my own destiny. Alone and wrapped up in myself, I determined to know nothing but this ship and no one else but Mischa.

Each afternoon, Mischa and I entered the plush recreation hall on the upper deck, and feeling like royalty, we played checkers. While playing checkers one afternoon, we heard some serious news on the radio from Israel. Even with everyone silent in the recreation room, we barely made out the words that came across the ocean with crackling static. "Adolf Eichmann who had been captured a year ago and smuggled to Israel from Argentina is waiting for trial."

Immediately, cheers and applauding came from different parts of the ship. Then groups of passengers huddled at a radio speaker nearest to them to hear the rest of the news. "Though Israel does not recognize capital punishment," we heard the announcer say, "a special law has now been formulated to hang the man responsible for the cruel deaths of millions of Jews in Europe." No one was applauding now. Silent tension filled the ship. It was at least two days before the atmosphere on board returned to its usual carefree cheerfulness.

After several days at sea, I began to crave the feel of solid ground under my feet, though the rocking of the ship did not disturb me. Certainly it did not affect me the way it apparently did a great many passengers. Early one morning I was awakened by a strange, forceful pressure to my head. Disoriented and helpless to move my body, I rolled my eyes around in an effort to get my bearings. *The ship is toppled over,* I told myself, *I'm upside down.* The pressure kept increasing. The top of my head pulsated. *So much for getting to America,* I relented, and just then the pressure let up and I slid, blankets and all, until my feet pressed against the footboard of my bunk. It took a moment to realize that I had not been upside down. *A storm! I better go tell Mischa.*

Realizing that I was alone, I struggled off the bunk, staggered out the door and was shocked by the sight of about two dozen people assuming unusual positions. Many were sitting on the floor of the long corridor, some were lying down, others, stooping. All looked pathetic. Several were moaning and some were heaving into little bags with *Zion* on them. Still others quietly endured seasickness. I assumed that they were all waiting for the rest rooms, but I was sure most never would make it in.

Ignoring these undignified unfortunates, I knocked on Mischa's door. It opened immediately.

"I expected your knock," he said. "I'm the only one left in here." After sizing up the situation in the corridor, he cheerfully added, "Let's go to the dining hall for breakfast!"

We waded through the maze of people to make our way to a deserted dining room. What did fill the room was the overpowering aroma of freshly baked breakfast rolls; on each of the twenty or so tables they lay in large, mounded basketfuls. Along with the rolls, three types of cheese and an array of condiments awaited appetites. A uniformed waiter offered us eggs any style and a choice of four beverages. Usually, we had no such choices. It felt good to me to see no people around, for I was too self-conscious to enjoy eating in public. We felt like pampered dignitaries, chuckling about being alone with the waiters solely at our service. We wished we could have had an endless appetite, so as not to waste all the abandoned food.

When we felt we could eat no longer, we tottered out of the dining hall, still feeling the floor teetering under our feet. In spite -- or perhaps because -- of the storm, we were ready to tackle the day's activities, wondering why nearly everyone in the lower deck was sick. *We* were having a joyride!

Mischa and I were used to this kind of balancing act from countless wildly driven bus rides. Even then, we made it a game of skill, balancing like surfers while everyone else held on for dear life. Proud that he wasn't seasick, Mischa sprang into a hand stand. Like an acrobat, he walked on his hands the width of the large dance floor in front of the dining hall, well in sight of the unfortunates. He always was the clown of the crowd. I was proud of him.

About midway through the two-week voyage, the crew joined all passengers to celebrate Israel's thirteenth Independence Day out on the main deck. Disappointed by the short, uneventful ceremony of raising the Israeli flag and singing the national anthem, I thought of her for the first time since we left. *She is no longer my country.* Yet I felt an annoying emptiness at this occasion, a poor and indifferent substitute without parades, folk dancing on the streets and fireworks. It felt like a commemoration of her death rather than her rebirth. Perhaps that was best for me. I could not afford, at this point, to feel homesick. Nevertheless, I thought she deserved much more celebration.

Sea and more sea. But today we looked forward to ten hours on solid ground as we approached the port of Naples, Italy. Would we want to depart or remain on board, was the question. Of course we wanted to leave, in spite of the rain. This was Italy! We felt eight feet tall -- even I.

As soon as we stepped off the gangplank we were confronted by a toothless old merchant with a cart full of luscious fresh fruit. Quite cleverly, I thought, Mischa managed to bargain with him, via sign language. After all, Italians and Jews have their flying, flinging hands in common, not to mention the enjoyment of a good sale or a good bargain!

While munching our snack and getting wet from the

drizzle, we were approached by another cocky old man with a horse and open carriage at his side. We considered ourselves accomplished Italian bargainers, if only twenty steps old, as Mischa again talked the price down with determination for a ride through Naples. A bus tour was, for us, financially out of the question.

Into the back of the carriage we hopped and we were off to see some of the most beautiful sights our eyes had witnessed. The seaport, with its graceful curve, resembled the one in Haifa, Israel. It was a breathtaking view. Ancient, picturesque buildings, intricately carved and sculptured fascinated us and challenged our artistic tastes. Some we liked, some we hated; at all of them we marvelled.

Our driver kept shouting out words with astonishing speed while pointing to specific buildings and sights. He knew we were unable to understand him, but it was obviously a memorized tour presentation he felt obligated to give for the fee. It hardly mattered. We chuckled at his cocky-sounding words and enjoyed the ride.

I slept wonderfully that night, tired out and filled with memories of the adventure of our lives.

Then came Marseille, France, a few days later, where we also went ashore for more adventure. Off we stepped from the gangplank onto French soil, soggy like Naples was, but not nearly as exciting to us.

Though we had very little money, we felt rich, adventurous and daring. To our dismay, it rained the entire day. Getting wet, however, did not discourage our journey through the streets. Alleys were decorated with smelly trash cans where alley cats lived, ate, and fought. We felt good, ignoring our soggy clothes, walking as long and as far as our feet would carry us. No horse and carriage rescued us here; no fruit merchant challenged our bargaining ability. It was a gray, foggy day. Not a soul was there to dull the agony I felt during the inevitable conversation we resorted to while walking.

"Mischa, what's it going to be like in America?" I dared to ask for the first time.

"Imma tells me in the letters that everyone has the opportunity to advance and become 'somebody.' I will try to get a job as a dental technician and become independent as soon as possible."

"And leave me alone with Imma and Jim?"

"By that time, Yaffa, you'll feel at home, have school friends and will not need me at all."

"But I *do* need you, Mischa; how can you say that? You are the only person I will really know and be able to trust in a strange, big country. It's so scary to imagine. I try not to think about it."

"Think of it as our last chance to live a family life, and a very fortunate opportunity to pull out of poverty. In America anyone can make a lot of money, and I intend to do exactly that. No more welfare for me!"

"It's easy for you to say. What am *I* supposed to do while you're busy being independent? I don't even know what to say to Imma... I dread the first day with her. And Jim, what should I say to him? He speaks only English and Polish."

"I am sure everything will work out fine, awkward at first, but we must have hope, Yaffa. This is our last chance. Now look around, this is France!"

"Yes, we are just like rich American tourists. We even

have a camera,'' I joked back.

"Not rich yet, but you just wait and see." At that moment, a cat jumped out of a trash can near us and darted out of sight, ruining our make-believe rich tourist act.

"There's nothing worthwhile to take a picture of here, it's too foggy," said Mischa. "Let's turn in to another street. This one looks and smells too much like the slums where we used to live. I've had enough of that!"

"Yes, I've had enough, too," I echoed. "I have tried my best to forget the past. It's so difficult to keep from thinking about some of it without knowing something about the future." Mischa, my mentor, had nothing to say this time, no solutions, no wise answers.

The air between us was beginning to feel uncomfortably quiet. Without the excitement we felt in Italy, we were forced to face the uncertainty of our future.

"Mischa, I'm getting too tired to walk any more. Can we go back to the ship?" I broke the silence.

Two days after France we reached the great Rock of Gibraltar. It had been the talk of the passengers. Out on the main deck, Mischa and I marveled as our vessel snail-pacedly "squeezed" through the narrow passageway. There were moments when we held our breaths, sure that the ship was too wide to make it through. Once we passed the rocks, we sighed in relief. We felt as if we had just been funneled through from the Mediterranean into the Atlantic. Mischa took plenty of pictures to prove we had been there.

After Gibraltar there was nothing but blue ocean all the way -- no more stops, no adventures. During this second part of the voyage I was getting restless, realizing how much I missed my mountains and fields where I could hike and pick flowers. Even the sounds of merchants shouting through the streets and dogs barking at them, I would have welcomed now. To keep from getting bored, I captured in my senses the distinctive sounds and sights on the ship.

"Swish-splat... swish-splat," went the ever present rhythm of sea. As the ship carved the waters, sassy ripples frothed and slapped its side. All day; all night, the swish-splat, swish-splat sound never missed a beat, while the engine competed for its lead song of constant monotone.

I paid a price for such nautical entertainment. Out on the deck, a salty mist arose with vengeance every time and sprayed my face, choking away my breath and burning my eyes. I never could stay there long, but braved it every day.

Mischa and I were having the adventure of our lives. We could now tell the world we had been to Italy, France, and crossed the Mediterranean and the Atlantic! Despite the monotony, I thoroughly enjoyed the fifteen-day voyage, hoping with all my heart that it wouldn't come to an end. I knew that when it did, the uncertain future would confront me.

Last day aboard ship. Nervously, I packed and repacked my two suitcases repeatedly, merely to pass the time. During the last hour I could no longer contain myself and began to pray. *If only I could have a family,* I confided with desperate longing. *Nothing fancy, just a mother, a father, Mischa and I. Maybe, just maybe you can make it come true. This is our last chance, God,* I reminded Him, fighting back the tears.

*I must not leave here sad,* I thought. In defiance of my bleak-looking future, I set out to prove to myself that I was willing to be a "new" person in a new country. Solemnly, almost ceremoniously, I set my tooth retainer on the bathroom sink, and left it there. Suppressing my guilt over leaving behind Mischa's skillful, top quality work, I took a last look in the mirror to see the progress my teeth had made. *Good enough,* I rationalized, and marched out bravely.

Mischa had been standing on the deck with his camera, eager to capture the long awaited Statue of Liberty. His eye still in the lens, he spoke to me like a radio announcer, "Here we are, Yaffa, in New York, America! What is the first thought that comes to your mind?"

"Hope," I dramatized, playing a distinguished tourist. "And what, sir, are your first words?"

Mischa looked away from the camera, toward foggy New York as our Israeli ship *Zion* entered the harbor. "America, here we come!" he shouted as the sudden blast of the ship's horn helped announce our arrival.

*chapter fourteen*

# *English for French*

**In New York,** we were met by the Hermans, who lived with us in our first stone house in Yaffo, and recently emigrated. This arrangement was made by Aunt Marga. When our baggage was finally cleared, Mr. Herman drove us to their apartment.

As we stepped out of the car, gray, foggy air and uninviting darkness created by the tall skyscrapers were a disappointment. I had been accustomed to open, blue skies nine months out of the year. New York's atmosphere reminded me of Marseille, only this was worse, not at all new-looking to me. *How could this be America, the land of the rich?* My first impression of America did nothing for my confidence that things would turn out all right.

I scarcely remembered the Hermans, for I was four years old when I last saw them. Reverting to my typical bashfulness, I answered only when the questions seemed urgent. Here, for the first time since we left Israel, we spoke

Hungarian, our only common language with them. Mischa and Mr. Herman chatted incessantly. Mrs. Herman attempted to make conversation with me. Gazing at me for a moment, she said, "You've grown, Yaffa." I detected her omission of "how much" at the beginning of this near-compliment, and the absence of a pleasantly surprised tone at the end. At fourteen and a half I measured a mere four feet seven inches and weighed seventy-six pounds. My reaction to her was my usual downcast stare. Next she said, "You look weary," and offered me their full-sized bed.

I had never seen one, nor had I ever laid eyes on such an "unnecessary" thing as a box spring. The tall bed did look inviting, however, and I nodded in acceptance. We had a flight to make at midnight. This was one o'clock in the afternoon. Timidly, I went to bed, and with the door closed behind me, fell asleep for ten hours.

When I awoke, it was time to get ready for the airport. Mischa and Mr. Herman were still talking. Mrs. Herman refrained from trying to speak to me. I must have exasperated her before going to sleep.

I was excited about flying in a jet airplane, yet my excitement was jumbled with the unpleasant past and the uncertain future. I couldn't sort out anything. *Why was I here?* All I felt was butterflies in my stomach.

En route to California, our plane stopped in Chicago, around four in the morning. I was just dozing off again when Mischa nudged me saying, "We have an hour, would you like to see Chicago?" He expected me to jump at the opportunity.

Sleepily, I looked out into the darkness. "Chicago?" I mumbled, "No, I just want to go back to sleep. I don't care about Chicago,'' and dozed off to awaken in sunny California.

At approximately seven in the morning California time, we arrived at Oakland Airport where my mother and a friend waited beside a car. As my mother didn't drive, this was a favor on the part of her friend, Mrs. Smith. It made the reunion more awkward for me.

''Shalom,'' said my estranged mother in Hebrew, as was our custom in Israel, regardless of what language we were using. Then in Hungarian, she continued, ''Welcome to America. Did you have a pleasant trip?''

Hoping Mischa would do all the talking and answering, I merely nodded, ''yes,'' and cringed as she tried to hug me. No one, including my mother was going to hug me, especially in front of another stranger. I was not in a huggable mood; neither was I in a talkative one. I just wanted to disappear from the face of the earth. The butterflies in my stomach must have grown larger, for I could scarcely swallow. Even my throat pulsated. I was unprepared to deal with my new life.

In the car I wondered why Jim, my mother's husband, had not come to pick us up. As though sensing my question, my mother said, ''Jim had a tooth extracted yesterday. His face is swollen and painful, so he stayed home.''

*Just as well with me,* I thought coldly and leaned against the door of the back seat staring aimlessly out the window. *I am here,* I told myself, *and there is nothing I can do about it. ''We must have hope, Yaffa,''* Mischa's voice echoed in my mind.

''Tenk you, Mrs. Smit,'' said my mother with her heavy, unmistakably Hungarian accent.

We left the car and entered an ancient apartment house on sixth avenue in East Oakland. It looked like a mansion to me. Inside, Jim was standing in the kitchen with an ice bag on his cheek. He awkwardly greeted Mischa with a hand shake. When my turn came, he ignored my outstretched hand, leaving me embarrassed and uncomfortable. Then he turned around and walked away, in pain, no doubt. It took a lot of courage for me to extend my hand. I wanted terribly to make a good first impression, but instead, felt unwelcome.

From the first day on, Jim and I did not get along. We all clashed, and in no time, daily arguments and fights over ridiculous matters dominated our "family life."

One of these arguments was over "mopping." I was intrigued with a gadget I had never seen before, the sponge mop. Several times a day, I mopped the floors, not necessarily out of helpfulness, but rather out of playfulness. This angered Jim, who thought I should be washing dishes instead. Though my mother was willing to let me mop to my heart's content, Jim's yelling at her for doing so created so much daily tension, that I began avoiding him.

Another source of contention was my very limited English. One day, responding to something Jim said to me, I mistakenly said "I do" instead of "I know." He laughed and mocked this error until I was in tears. His unreasonable criticism of my English caused me to keep silent again. I resolved never to speak an English word outside of school until I was confident with the language, and made no mistakes. Tenaciously, I fulfilled this resolve.

Sitting at my contact paper-covered desk unable to concentrate on my homework one afternoon, I shoved the books out of my way, exasperated. "Nothing works out for me in life!" I threw up my arms angrily. Then I thought of my dear friend Ilka in Israel. I had promised to write to her. She was probably waiting for my letter now, hoping to receive some happy news from me. *Nothing of the kind could happen! I have no good news for her,* I thought.

Ilka, the only daughter of doting Hungarian parents, friends of Aunt Marga, was two years my elder. Our short friendship during my stay at Aunt Marga's was an emotional one.

Occasionally, Aunt Marga visited Ilka's parents and I came along. They lived close to the ocean, an hour's bus ride away. When Ilka and I began to talk, it centered around my sad life. Her "sisterly" love toward me opened my heart in a way no one else could before. It was a sad day when we came to Ilka's home so I could say goodbye to her.

In my arms I carried a sack. In it was my most prized possession, a beautiful, large, American doll. My mother sent it to me from America while I was still at the orphanage.

During all my childhood I had owned only one other doll, but for merely a day. Father had brought it home while he was in the navy in Yaffo, to make up for his absence. Proud of my new rag doll, I ran out of our one-room abode to meet my friend Lisa. When Lisa saw the doll, she jealously pulled at her arm, while I held on to her with all my strength. With Lisa pulling one arm, and I, the other, my brand new doll was rent in two.

In the orphanage, my second doll became very important to me, even at age twelve. Now, at fourteen, I was still attached to this beautiful doll of Elizabeth Taylor in a wedding gown.

"I'll miss you, little Yaffa," said Ilka with a tender smile.

Not having the courage to reply to such an emotional statement, I pulled out the sack from under my arm. "Here, this is for you. I can't take her with me because she is too big."

"Oh, I couldn't take such an expensive, beautiful gift," she replied after opening the sack.

"You're the only person I know who deserves her. Please take good care of her, and remember me when you do."

"I'll take good care of her, thank you. Now, I have something for you, Yaffa. It's not as big or as expensive as your doll, but it's all I could think of."

Ilka handed me a recent photograph of herself, which she mounted on a heart-shaped piece of cardboard. On the back, neatly printed in Hebrew with red ink, it read: "To my little sister, Yaffa, to remember me by. With love, from your sister forever, Ilka."

Only Ilka's genuine love could provoke me to tears, and while I could not and did not know how to thank her, we embraced for a short moment. I wanted to cry in her arms, but stopped myself.

"Goodbye, little sister," she choked on her words.

"I'll never forget you," I replied with a quiver in my voice.

*Sisters forever,* I thought, as we left her home.

*I will write to her now,* I decided, coming back to the present.

"Dear Ilka," I wrote in Hebrew, "I know you have been waiting to hear how I am doing in America. It's no use pretending. Since I've been here, I have experienced so many disappointments, it would take a book to write about them. Even now, as I am crying, my tears are falling on the paper. Ilka, I can't bear it here, and I see no solutions."

A few weeks after I sent the letter, came Ilka's reply. "I am sorry to read that you are so unhappy, and that the family life you so wanted didn't work out. I am crying for you, Yaffa, just as I always did when you told me about your life. Why don't you do what you said, write a book, your life-story, and send it to me for my seventeenth birthday, coming up in two months. It would be the best gift anyone could give me."

I was fifteen by now, and the thought of recalling all those horrible incidents in Israel, which I was desperately trying to forget, did not appeal to me at all. Since it was Ilka's request, however, I went right to work the next day.

Even with concentrated daily writing after school, often instead of homework, the book didn't make it for Ilka's birthday. Complete with illustrations, the handwritten Hebrew book, entitled, "Chronicles of My Life," arrived four months past her birthday.

"Yaffa," wrote Ilka after reading the book, "Whenever I feel depressed, I pick up your book and start reading it. Then I realize I am the luckiest girl in the world!"

While I was glad that my book served some good purpose in Ilka's life, the knowledge did nothing to alleviate, or even ease the pain in my situation here in America.

The particular junior high I attended had a special program for foreign students, with teachers who specialized in helping us foreigners catch up in the English language, and to adjust to American ways. From the first day in school, I was hearing various languages spoken by groups of students belonging to their respective ethnic backgrounds: Chinese, Spanish, Portuguese, Japanese, Dutch, Hindi, Filipino, Persian, Greek, and more. They all fascinated me, as I had always enjoyed listening to foreign languages. Since no one else in school was from Israel, I heard no Hebrew outside of Mischa. Consequently, I felt more alone than ever, regressing, as I did at kindergarten and elementary school in Israel. The extent of my regression was becoming an embarrassment even to myself, like on my first day.

As I was led into the special classroom by a staff member, my behavior was no less childish than it was when I entered public school in Haifa. Too nervous to respond to my teacher's greeting, I merely stood in front of her, gazing tensely at the floor. Then the teacher turned to the class, saying something I didn't understand, except that she mispronounced my name. This was the first time I had ever heard my name said with an "American" accent.

A girl from India, with long, dark braided hair raised her hand in response to the teacher. Then, the teacher, whom I now understood to be Mrs. McDonald, took me over to be seated beside her. Immediately, this girl began to instruct me, disregarding both the lesson and the teacher, how to write numbers and form English letters. Apparently she volunteered to help orientate me by giving me personal instruction for which the teacher had no time.

Not understanding her English, which even to my foreign ear sounded distorted, I felt just like I did in Israel when a classmate was determined to teach me to speak. As much as

I would have liked to, I couldn't respond to her very patient instruction.

In India, numbers as well as letters are different from those used in America. The girl assumed that since I was unfamiliar with English handwriting, neither did I know numbers.

Like a parent, she took my hand in hers, and with a pencil slowly moved it to form the numbers. Humiliated among some students who ignored the teacher to listen in on my "tutor's" instructions, I jerked my hand from under hers and silently refused to continue.

*I know numbers,* I thought angrily. *Being dropped two grade levels is embarrassing enough. I will not subject myself to being treated like a kindergartner!*

Then came the Alphabet, a few days later. With a sharp pencil and plenty of practice paper, the Indian girl, whose name I could never pronounce, took my hand again, speaking softly as to a frightened child. Skillfully, she slid my hand across the paper to form the letters "a," "b," "c."

Hungarian uses the same alphabet as does English. I knew how to print since the time I taught myself to read and print in lower case from Father's Hungarian newspapers at age six. What I was being shown that day, however, was handwriting, which I had dreamed of being able to do for many years. Seeing the slight difference between this and my awkward, self-taught printing, I suddenly became fascinated and, therefore, cooperative.

Surprised and pleased with my unexpected response, the girl quickly switched to numbers again, hoping to interest me in them, while pointing to the math problems on the blackboard. Angered by her trickery, I seized the pencil, copied the first problem from the board. With all the speed I could manage, I solved it without blinking an eye. *There!* I told her mentally, *now can you see that I don't need lessons in writing numbers?*

After this, my Indian tutor gave up on me, asking to be relieved of her task. Eventually, I adjusted to the newness of my American school, but craved more mental stimulation than I was getting at the sixth grade level.

On one occasion I went to my counselor and asked, "Please, can I learn French?"

"I'm sorry, she replied, "We don't allow more than one foreign language at a time. Perhaps by the time you get to high school, you'll know English well enough to study another language.

"Two more years too long for me," I protested, "I want learn French now."

There was no way I would have convinced her of my sincere desire to begin my French studies before reaching high school. I wanted to have two years of it by then.

The French language became an obsession, and I was determined to major in it as I grew older. But I wasn't getting any help or encouragement here. Though I could make myself understood, I couldn't use convincing language.

Disappointed, I determined to learn English twice as fast. I wanted to be transferred to the regular curriculum, where a foreign language (other than English) was required. After all, it was my lack of knowledge of the English language that set me back two years. Logically, I figured that by accelerating my English, I should be able to enter high school at least a year before my allotted time. It was more English, or no French.

It worked! In a short six weeks, the remainder of that school year, my English vocabulary had soared above and beyond the expected. Soon I passed even the Indian girl who was my personal tutor during my first two weeks. Mrs. McDonald, pleased with my progress, recommended I be skipped to my proper grade level, but continue in a "foreign" English class for one period a day throughout high school. I could graduate from junior high after the six-week period. I was skipped from the end of sixth to the end of eighth grade in a few weeks, as though I had been in eighth grade all year.

During the summer months, I diligently continued to increase my English vocabulary by working crossword puzzles, devouring dictionaries, and watching television.

Television, my new fascination, was my only listening source of English conversation at home, for Jim and I were no longer on speaking terms. It also served as a convenient escape from daily family arguments.

*chapter fifteen*

# No Jesus for Me!

**I was standing in the kitchen** cringing. *Is this the beginning of another Saturday morning family fight?* Sure enough, a few words of contention abruptly burst into a full-fledged brawl. Jim was hurling insults at my mother; my mother was hurling dishes at Jim. Mischa was vigorously exercising his "gift" of peacemaking, shouting orders to them both, then forcefully pushing them apart, only to see them pouncing on each other again. No peace was imminent.

In the heat of it all, I saw my mother remove a saucepan off a red-hot burner and aim its contents -- scalding milk -- toward Jim. I knew it was safer for me to evacuate the kitchen, but I was too stunned to move. So was Jim! At that exact moment, someone knocked at the front door. Everyone froze. I wanted to scurry to another room to avoid meeting the knocker, but, alas, he opened the door and walked right in.

Mortified, I fled to the dining room, grabbed the wall behind me and clung to it, as if to protect it. It was a desperate, urgent reaction. I knew -- we all knew -- the man heard the fight. As for me, fear of this person turned the stress of the fight into a feeling of reproach.

With a cheerful "hello" and a bright smile, this man seated himself at the dining table directly across from me. My mother was busying herself at the sink, obviously too embarrassed to face him. Mischa and Jim vanished into the T.V. room.

"What a pleasant surprise, Ruth!" he addressed my mother, but directed his penetrating steel-blue eyes at me. Quickly I cast my own eyes at my bare feet, making sure I could still see him.

"Yes, she here now, Mr. Yates," came my mother's shocking reply, as if they both planned on my presence.

"So this is your long lost daughter from Israel," he said, and then committed the act I dreaded and wished to avoid in the first place. "Nice to meet you, finally," he spoke to me. "I helped your mother write some letters in English in regards to your immigration. I also communicated with her attorney. You see, I have an investment in you." The word "investment" was unfamiliar to me, but the sound of it I committed to memory, to research later.

*He's known my mother,* I thought. *He calls her by first name, opens the door himself and seats himself.* These are signs of a reasonably longstanding friendship by European standards. His accent was distinctly European, but unlike my mother's. *Who is he? What is he doing here, and why is he pretending to be so happy?*

Unaffected by my unnatural and inappropriate posture at

the wall, Mr. Yates continued to speak to me. With my limited English, I understood the bulk of what he was saying, but was unable to formulate English thoughts. My internal translating process overworked, I became frustrated. As was my habit, I intended to say nothing to this stranger, anyway.

Gentlemanly yet forward was the way he came across, and he wasted no time admitting that he came to tell me about God.

"Jesus is our Messiah -- *your* Messiah -- and friend." he emphasized.

Instant stomach-churning disgust came over me. *What! How dare he tell me such abominations.* Though spitting was unfitting at my age, and in front of this stranger, the urge was certainly, and almost instinctively, there. I made sure my face expressed my feelings while I carried on a silent argument within.

"Surely you need a friend," he insisted, "You can trust God. He loves you so much that He sent His son, Jesus, to die on the cross..." I winced.

*Absurd! A figure hanging on a cross, such as I detest, can neither be a friend, nor has it life to be able to die,* I argued internally in Hebrew.

*If only I could express myself in English, I would tell him a thing or two. How would he know whether I need a friend. It's none of his affair, anyway.*

"Jesus came to the Jews first, and they rejected him."

*Good for them! I would have done the same. We have ONE God, no relatives. "Here O Israel, the Lord God is one God."* I consoled myself. *I can understand God being a friend, but Jesus? No. No Jesus for me!*

Paul Yates was kind, but annoyingly insistent. I wondered if he could see the anger welling up in me. He pushed it too far, I thought.

"If you don't believe what I am telling you, ask God Himself if He has a son," he challenged.

*Blasphemy! God doesn't answer people, He merely listens. Anyone who thinks he hears God speaking is mentally unstable.* How I wished to be able to verbalize my arguments now! I regretted having only one English word in my vocabulary to express what I thought of him. The spines of my prickly skin stood ready to prick with one more attempt to insult my intelligence.

Now he stared at me, knowing well he was "touching" more than my prickly exterior. What he said with this challenging yet compassionate stare, instead, pricked *me* to the core. I could bear it no longer. Momentary boldness replaced timidity. Self-righteousness overshadowed respect for my elders. Filled with contempt, letting go of the wall, I sprang toward him shouting, "You -- you, crazy!" Then I promptly returned to my former position, my heart pounding, my body nervously trembling.

*That ought to take care of him!* I thought. *He'll never come back here again, thinking I am a sassy brat, not worth talking to.* I took a deep breath to slow down my racing heart, sure that I offended the man.

I didn't. He never scowled, nor did my "disrespect" change his attitude toward me. Instead, with more love and compassion in his eyes than before, he provoked me to listen.

I hated every word he uttered. Yet this man himself, I could no longer hate.

He left, at last, the man with the crazy story, who dared to tell my mother at the door, "Make sure to bring her to the Friday meeting."

I tried desperately to forget the entire incident. I had my share of the Christian religion. *Why is it following me half a world away? Why is it coming up eleven years after I was persecuted by "Christians" in my own Jewish country?* My religion, I felt, was a personal matter.

I had nearly forgotten the incident with Paul Yates until the next Friday, when I found myself accompanying my mother to his home. With belligerent curiosity, I was determined to "spy" in on this meeting, to see where my mother had been lured.

It was evening. There were perhaps twenty other Jewish faces smiling at us as I was being introduced. Obviously, my mother knew the people. *Has she lost her Jewish pride? What an abomination!* I screamed inside. Disgust was suddenly competing with my self-consciousness. Two people moved over on a long couch and gestured for us to sit. Reluctantly, I positioned myself next to my mother.

A too-sweet-looking elderly lady inched her way toward a piano. We were handed songbooks as she struck piano keys and carefully studied the notes before her, as if they were unfamiliar to her.

With his eyes bright and mouth opened wide, Paul Yates bellowed out a familiar melody that caught my attention. The tune was the Israeli national anthem, *Hatikva* (The Hope). I hadn't heard it since the ship *Zion*. The words were English. *Someone dared write Christian lyrics to my sacred Jewish anthem!* Unable to read fast enough to follow the singing, I merely pretended, defiantly singing the original Hebrew words. Were I able to follow the words, I would not have "disgraced" myself to Christian words. Paul Yates gazed at me, as if to say, "This one's for you, the Israeli among us."

Against my will, my eyes became transfixed upon Mr. Yates, and I hoped he wouldn't notice. Every word he sang with his charming accent, which by now I recognized to be Polish, was full of life.

By the time the third song was over, with all my mind I was fighting the possible reason why twenty or so Jewish people and one too-sweet-to-be-real gentile would subject themselves to such a meeting.

My train of thought was interrupted by the enthusiastic voice of Mr. Yates who was now speaking, welcoming everyone. The loud, Jewish chatter suddenly ceased, and Mr. Yates began what I considered a Christian speech. The words reminded me of my unpleasant confrontation with him the previous week. In my effort to comprehend his words, my eyes became again fixed upon his lively, happy Jewish countenance. He spoke for an eternity, and when the speech was over, the loud Jewish chatter continued as if it were never interrupted.

All were standing now. I had missed the invitation to another room for refreshments, probably because I was concentrating too much. Slowly, noisily, two long tables were surrounded. A prayer was begun. It sounded harmless to me until the end. The instant I heard, "in Jesus' name." I shuddered. Anger and indignation welled up within me. Memories of past persecution and injustices flooded my mind. *I never should have come to America; I never should have come here!*

Sitting at the table, reluctantly picking at a cookie and sipping some tea, I could scarcely believe that a Jewish man would give a Christian speech, and make such a fuss over his beliefs. As my mind kept returning to what I was taught in the convent, it occurred to me that I saw neither statues nor other Catholic symbols in the house. Rather, a brass *menorah*, the seven-branched candelabra, Israel's national symbol, adorned the mantle. *What an unthinkable paradox!*

The hour was getting late when most of the people had made their exits with warm greetings, inundated with Jewish hugs and kisses. Mr. Yates just waited patiently, and then drove several of us back home. My mother and I exchanged not a word during or after the meeting.

*Never again!* I promised myself in the car. *I am Jewish! What's more, an Israeli, and should not be attending a meeting like this.*

The impression that Paul Yates had left on me was unshakable. It haunted me at school, on the way home and while doing homework. Leaving my resolution at home, somehow I found myself at the Yates' home a week later, and a week after that, and every Friday for the next three years. Yet, the war was on. It was between his claims and my internal rebuttals. To each meeting I came armed for battle with a pad and pen. In it, I secretly recorded my angry arguments in Hebrew. It was a safe secret for no one else there knew Hebrew. My strategy was to confound Mr. Yates with "the truth" once I became more proficient in English. From the second meeting on, I never came without my retaliation pad, and without reminding myself that I hated the name of Jesus and all that Christianity represented to me. On the other hand, I couldn't stay away from the meetings, never willing to admit that, for some unexplainable reason, I still enjoyed them.

When school mates asked me what I was doing on Friday nights, I made excuses for attending the meetings. Most gave me a puzzled look and questioned, ''You're giving up a party for a religious meeting?''

''Well, I go there, but don't you think for one minute that I believe anything of what is said!'' I always assured.

With my mind I was fighting what I heard at the meetings, telling myself, *No one can convince me, a Jew of Israeli stock, to believe that a man named Jesus came to his own people to... how do they put it... redeem them and bring them back to God. And Mr. Yates can harp till he's blue in the face that this... Messiah loves me and wants to be my friend.* The notes on my retaliation pad said that this was impossible, untrue, and un-Jewish.

*chapter sixteen*

# High School

**Life, as miserable as it was** for me, had to go on, so I concentrated on putting my schoolwork in first place among my varied interests. High school was a breeze for me, and my dream of studying French had been realized. The high school administration decided that it would be to my benefit to remain in the foreign program with the exception of two subjects. These I spent in regular American classes to help me assimilate. Fortunately, one of those was my French class.

In the foreign program, this time with over two hundred other students from at least fifteen countries, one of our special teachers was a six-foot-four Mormon from Utah. His accent was sometimes difficult for us to understand. Mr. Worthington was more of a friend to us than a teacher. He was dedicated to the cause of helping us make it in the American society, as well as to the cause of helping Americans accept us. For this reason, he formed a traveling entertainment group. It involved those who had a talent in bringing out the flavor of their nationality, through songs, dances or both. Several times Mr. Worthington tried to get me involved in this group, but I refused out of fear. One day after school, he spent nearly an hour telling me how much my Hebrew folk songs and Israeli folk dances would enhance the program. I finally agreed, and with surprising commitment became part of the show. We performed before other schools in the county, as well as in many other counties. In time we even entertained at adult clubs, where foreign or humanitarian interests made our show appropriate. Mr. Worthington spent many tireless hours with us after school, rehearsing and putting together new and fresh programs. For once I felt worthwhile, being in a position where teachers and students alike appreciated what I had to give them.

Soon I became so much part of the "foreign cause" that Americans seemed like the foreigners to me. Mr. Worthington always made it a point to encourage us to mix by bringing up his observations and experiences. Often our English or social studies lessons would turn into his reminiscences and advice. Yet we loved him, because he loved to talk any time, anywhere, about anything. He also loved to laugh.

"Worthington" was a difficult name for most of the foreign students to pronounce, so there were nearly as many versions to his name as there were nationalities. One winter morning, I was seated next to a Hungarian-born Jewish girl from Belgium, who giggled at anything out of the ordinary. I happened to be in a playful mood (unusual for me). Leaning over toward her, I whispered in Hungarian,

"Mariana, look at Mr. Worthington's big foot, do you see something funny?"

"Which one? He's got two big feet, one on the floor and the other on the chair... Oh, no!"

Mariana burst into uncontrollable laughter. It spread through the entire class. By now Mr. Worthington's face was beet-red, realizing we were laughing at something to do with him. With his good nature and sense of humor that made us free to laugh at him, he stopped the lesson saying, "All right, class! Let me in on this. What's so funny, maybe I can laugh with you?"

No one had the nerve to tell him, for we loved him too much to insult him.

"C'mon, I can take it; someone tell me what's wrong with me."

Looking at one another, all eyes stayed on Mariana, bravest and boldest among us. She also rolled her "r's" forcefully, as Hungarians do.

"Mr. Vellington," Mariana started, then gulped, blushed, and spoke with obvious European diplomacy, "Yourrh socks, dey are two differrent colorrh. I am so sorry to tell you, but it vas verry funny."

"Oh?" Mr. Worthington glanced at his feet, now both on the floor, and forced a laugh, "Ha, ha, ha. I guess you're right, that would be funny to someone else, but embarrassing to me. Let me tell you how it happened. You see, I live in Walnut Creek, an hour and a half from here. For me to make it in time, I get up when it's still dark outside. So, half asleep, I reach for anything in my drawer that feels like socks and put them on. Usually, my wife helps me with the colors of my socks and clothes because I am color blind, but she is away this week. Shows you how much I need her. Once in Utah, my wife and I..." The rest of the period was spent listening to another one of Mr. Worthington's experiences. We loved it, because it prevented us from having to listen to the lesson.

Another afternoon, Mr. Worthington announced that he had something serious to tell us. His voice sounded troubled, coming across with a tone of disappointment.

"I was distressed today at lunch when I walked into the student cafeteria and saw most of you there. Now, I have often shared with you in the past that no one can learn English if he does not practice it. What I saw in the cafeteria was, almost without exception, students with the same ethnic background in small cliques. Remember what cliques are?"

Some of us nodded in response, wondering what he was trying to tell us.

"They were yakking," he said, moving his thumb and index finger together and apart a few times to make his point.

"There was only one foreign person who mingled with other ethnic groups. For a while she was with the Chinese, then with the Mexicans and finally with a Portuguese girl. I watched her carefully. Do you know who this person is?"

Everyone looked around and there was a suppressed murmur for a moment until Mr. Worthington dropped the bomb.

"There she is," he pointed his long finger at me, and my heart practically jumped out of my body. "Yaffa has not a friend here from Israel. She cannot speak Hebrew to anyone. (He forgot I spoke Hungarian with Mariana.) As a result, she became a friend to anyone of you who would speak to her. I consider her the most sociable student in our program."

It was obvious he dramatized this incident to drive a lesson home. I hadn't realized that my "mingling" with various nationalities was noticeable. What Mr. Worthington was unaware of was that I had gone from one group to another because no one acknowledged me in any group. Indeed, there were cliques, and since they ignored my presence, I merely circulated. Listening in on the different languages was my joy, anyway.

"How about some of you trying to do the same, and socialize with other ethnic groups. That will be your homework for the next two weeks, announced our teacher.

"Aw, Mr. Wortinkten, that's not fair," complained a Filipino boy.

"Det's right, Mr. Worzington, we want to be widz' our friends; we used to dzem," protested a girl from Holland.

"It's all settled," he declared with hands in the air. "I know what you want, but it doesn't help you learn English. When you speak as well and as clearly as Yaffa, who has been in America less years than many of you, then you can speak your own language all you want. Back home in Utah, there were few foreigners, and..." Another back-home story lasted the rest of that period.

We spent many hours in similar ways, learning of Mr. Worthington's life rather than our lessons, but that only created the informal, unpretentious atmosphere unique to our class. It brought us closer to one another and to this teacher who was our friend.

We had another special teacher. She was an older woman

from somewhere in the midwest. Her speech was also un-Californian. It seemed as if our special English teachers were always the hard ones to understand.

Mrs. Wilson doubled as our counselor. In order to go to her class or for counselling, we went down to the converted basement. The basement was largely restricted to the foreign students in an attempt to avoid persecution and harassment.

Dear Mrs. Wilson, how often she bailed us foreign students out of trouble, putting her job on the line. She was a motherly sort of a person, and all our petty problems were discussed with her. Occasionally, I would come to see her in the poorly lit basement office to talk about my future.

"Tell me about your plans; what do you want to prepare for in high school?"

"I don't know," I hesitated, "I like languages most, but I also like art. I wouldn't mind becoming a cartoonist. Then I enjoy writing, but I don't know how I would use that." Surprising myself, I blurted out, "I want to work with people too. Is there anything -- some type of work that can include all my interests?"

*Why didn't I think like I used to?* I reproved myself silently. *What's the matter with me? I don't like people.*

"There seems to be only one solution," she interrupted my train of thought, "some type of volunteer organization where you can put your talents to work. Why don't you sign up for a foreign aid program like Peace Corps which incorporates some of the languages you speak?"

Now I was certain I didn't like people. It was a mistake to even hint at such a thing. Picturing myself with strangers and being too self-conscience to do my job, I shuddered at the thought.

"I think I would rather be an interpreter for the United Nations. I have been thinking I should master a total of ten languages."

"Ten?" she gasped. "That is a lot of languages."

"I only have four more to go," I assured her.

"You needn't wait until you speak that many. It will take many years of concentrated study. In the meantime, you can still be useful with what you already know. Why don't you look in the vocational file at the library. Study to see what preparation and requirements you will need, and we'll go from there."

I went to the library that afternoon, anxious and delighted that, finally, I had a goal. Then I read about the job description and found, to my disappointment, that U.N. interpreters are isolated entirely. They are enclosed in sound proof glass booths listening to the delegates via headphones, and interpreting by microphone without contact or seeing faces. Now the thought of being surrounded by impersonal apparatus in an isolated booth was worse than having to face people.

My disappointment launched me into a massive research project on the United Nations and what it stood for. After two months of tapping every resource I could get my hand on, I decided that, politically, I disagreed with the U.N. I was not going to pursue that goal.

When I returned to Mrs. Wilson, she let me ramble on, hoping that perhaps one day I would be able to make up my mind. Meanwhile, she assigned for me a college preparatory curriculum with French as major and art as minor.

Despite my disappointment in the U.N., languages were

still on my mind. I took to studying Chinese from some of my Chinese friends, Dutch from my best friend, Sylvia, and was searching for someone to teach me Italian. It was not exactly a game with me. I was sincere about getting a head start on these languages while I had all the foreign help. Of course, they could never teach me more than the basics. Even so, United Nations or not, I was determined to become an interpreter, or at least a translator.

Little did I realize, then, that my personality was gradually undergoing some unexpected changes. I am sure that were it not for the bold struggle against the message of a personal Messiah, I would have remained my old shy, introverted self. My involvement with the Yates meetings literally shook my being inside out. I was now willing, without realizing why, to break through my protective wall. Now and then I spoke out, but still not without reservations. Inside my prickly pear skin, the fruit was beginning to grow.

# chapter seventeen

# *Hope*

**Mischa was getting married,** and I feared being left
with my mother and Jim. No one else knew exactly what my
home life was like or how the quarrels and fights affected
me. Soon, my mother announced her intentions of
divorcing. I sighed in relief thinking, *better to divorce than
for one of them to kill the other.* The end of my "family
life" had arrived, however distorted it was. Some *last
chance* this was!

My mother became a welfare recipient. I felt like I had
been there before. We were by no means as poor as we
were in Israel, but just as embarrassed. I was embittered,
and Mischa was not there to offer me words of hope.

With my mother and myself alone, our squabbles, and
sometimes physical fights, became more frequent, and these
not only on Saturday mornings. As a result I began spending
more time away from home, often calling Paul Yates for
some wisdom or consolation. He always obliged. At times

he would pick me up with his car and take me for a ride while we talked. I could no longer bear my lot alone, and shared it with him and Elizabeth.

In a way, I felt hypocritical when I enlisted help from the Yateses. I never let on the extent of my feelings and plans to confound them.

One day at the Yates' home, I complained of severe stomach irritation and heartburn. Since Mrs. Yates used to be a nurse, her advice was, "Tell your mother to take you to a doctor. If she doesn't, we'll talk to her."

In the doctor's office I was questioned about my family life. Soon the doctor asked me for a brief description of how I got along with my mother. Being aware of my stormy background, he probed further, and then concluded, "Yaffa, you have developed ulcers. I have never had such a young ulcer patient. From what I can gather, living with your mother is contributing to it." I nodded in agreement. "In my opinion," he continued cautiously and compassionately, "you'd be better off to return to Israel."

I told him that was impossible. He shrugged his shoulders and sighed as if that was his last and best advice, and placed me on a strict, bland diet.

My heart pricked, I was in a quandary. *How could I tell my mother what I just heard?* Even with all that she had done, I couldn't bring myself to insult her this much.

When I told the Yateses of the results of my visit to the doctor, they understood. I had nowhere to go, yet it was detrimental for me to stay with my mother. Mr. Yates, nearly in tears, said, "We want you to know that Elizabeth and I love you as if you were our daughter. You let us know if any trouble arises. We are praying for you daily that you will find rest in the God of Israel through Messiah.''

For the first time since I had known them, I was touched, affected by their sincerity. I broke down, something I never did, lamenting my lot in life, and my feeling of belonging to no one and in no place. Mr. Yates gave me an assignment, to read Psalm 22 when I got home. He promised to visit our home more often. Though he never expressed it, I knew it was to insure my safety.

''My God, my God, why have you forsaken me...'' I read, and immediately identified with the author of this heart-wrenching plea. For some reason, that statement, alone, brought comfort to my bewildered heart.

I graduated from high school with nearly straight A's, pleased that I succeeded in completing high school at seventeen instead of nineteen. Nineteen was the average graduation age of foreign students. I was also pleased with the two years of French I had behind me. This was my third summer in America, marking not only my academic victories but the start of life-changing experiences. The first six weeks of my transition between high school and college, I worked in a hospital with three college girls. The four of us were hired to chart the conclusions of a five-year study on the effects of smoking during pregnancy on infants. It was a fascinating job, for which I was paid well for someone just out of high school. Regrettably, when we finished charting, the job was over. My only consolation was that the Yates' summer camp was coming up.

Now I was facing a giant paradox. The more I fought what I heard about Jesus, the more I felt compelled to attend the meetings and summer camps. Still filling pages of my retaliation pad, I thought that time had come to say something. Perhaps I can confound these Jewish people who believe in an un-Jewish God. I was in no way convinced of the validity of Jesus as the Jewish Messiah. So I thought I should tell God Himself -- complain to Him, for surely, if He sees anything, He sees this! God must be appalled by the claims of Mr. Yates and the likes of him. Certainly *I* was appalled, and since I was getting emotionally attached to the Yateses, I wished to help them out of their delusion.

I had given myself three years to speak English well enough to hold my side of an argument. *As soon as camp is over,* I thought, *my pad and I are ready!*

Such thoughts occupied my mind at about eight o'clock in the evening during my third summer camp at Mt. Hermon, California. This was the last evening of two weeks, and the Yateses were once again disappointed that I was still resisting my chance to accept Jesus as Messiah.

And now, this last evening, after supper, my cabin-mate, a middle-aged Jewish woman insisted she had something urgent to tell me. Mr. Yates had given her a most difficult task, that of challenging my stubborn Israeli heart toward Christ. All along I could tell she had been making efforts, but to no avail. She had not been able to get past my prickly skin.

While both of us sat on her bed in the front room, she told me of her experiences in knowing the Messiah personally. Hour after hour went by with my mind working overtime. My inner struggle was becoming unbearably strong, but I could not bring myself to express it.

She could ask God in prayer, and He would answer, she dared to tell me. Among other things, she told of specific incidents that changed her life for the better, attributing the results to answered prayer.

As the woman spoke, I was thinking, weighing, and wondering. *Why would she sit in a stuffy old cabin with me, divulging her personal affairs with God?* I still could not believe that God spoke to her in a way that she could apply to her life. I wanted to run for my pad, but sat, still but angry.

Sweat began to form all over my body, my struggle was so intense. I became restless and inwardly impatient, then hot and flushed, though the night air outside was getting chilly. *I'm getting sick; I must be feverish.*

I thought I had heard it all, yet the woman went on. *Her last ditch effort,* I thought, *to fulfill her assignment.* I tried to get bored, and failed. Yet I sat there, expressionless, giving her no indication that her "last ditch effort" was gaining over me. *How could I, an Israeli, give in without a good, Jewish fight?*

As soon as I thought this, I recalled Mr. Yates frequently reminding me, "When I am weak, then I am strong" (II Corinthians 12:10b). "When you are your weakest," he said, "God gives you strength."

Sitting almost motionlessly, I was no longer able to think. Nothing the woman said made logical sense, yet my heart longed to understand it. The sound of her voice became meaningless syllables.

In the middle of her words I stood up and left her.

It was midnight. Without a word, I entered my room, leaving behind a baffled cabin-mate. Kicking the door shut, I threw myself upon my creaky bed, mentally and emotionally drained.

"Oh, God of Israel!... God of Abraham, Isaac, and Jacob," my heart cried secretly. "If it is wrong for me to accept this Jesus as my Messiah, then please, please don't let me do it. Give me strength, for I am weak." After four hours of challenging words, I was desperate to know the truth.

I sobbed helplessly, trusting my Jewish God to protect me from the un-Jewish act. The strength I was asking for, I thought, was the ability to endure the "brainwashed" feeling I had. But I wasn't even certain of what I meant. In an instant, I let go. Willingly I succumbed, placing myself at the mercy of my God, regardless of the consequences.

Never in my life had I felt closer to God, as if He were right next to me. No longer fighting with my mind, I was opening my heart in total surrender, and whispered, "O.K., Jesus (His name was agony to speak out), you win. I believe. You must be the Messiah and my friend. When I think of you or say your name, I feel God's presence."

I wanted to talk to God forever, to let Him know I needed His help, and yes, His friendship. My sobs turned into sighs and soon I was enveloped with His peace. I fell asleep, knowing that I had made the right decision, else God -- my Jewish God -- would have prevented me.

Next morning I awoke with a feeling of hope. Reliving the night before, I put all my troubles in the background. There just had to be more to life than what I had seen so far. Hopes raised between the phases of my life's calamities had so far all crumbled before my eyes. But this hope, stronger and more meaningful than them all, must last. What strength I felt! What strength I *had*, all for admitting my weakness.

I prayed again. In a few moments of silent surrender, I

understood that true strength was also true hope, and that I had always been satisfied with false hope. Mischa merely talked of hope, but now I *had* it. How I wished he could have it too!

This morning, departure day, leaving my packed suitcase on my bed, I made my way up the dirt trail to the kitchen. Each step reminded me of another aspect of last night's experience. Inner peace and a privileged sense of knowing God continued to accompany me. *Yes,* I thought, *Jesus is my friend.* I silently apologized for having considered him my enemy.

My mind reflected on Isaiah 53, where the suffering Messiah is depicted as enemy to those who wished to be rid of him. In tears I continued to climb uphill praying, "How could I have rebelled so long?" I used to want to flee when Mr. Yates read from Isaiah 53. I could never bear to listen.

Just before breakfast, Mr. Yates and my discouraged cabin-mate were engrossed in reading the Old Testament. They were unaware of my approaching the open door. I heard him encourage her, not to think of her two weeks of effort as futile. She had neither read nor quoted the Bible to me... perhaps that was the problem, they rationalized. As I stood there, still, I quickly entreated God, my Friend. "I wish Mr. Yates would read Isaiah 53 to me." I was now longing for the very words that sent me running out the room before.

No sooner had I completed my petition to God, than Mr. Yates, with his gentle, blue eyes, looked up. Seeing me, he said, "Good morning, Yaffa. Would you like me to read to you from Isaiah, chapter 53?" Hot tears stung their way down my sunburned face and I could only nod in reply, amazed that God granted my request so promptly. For the first time I realized that He *does* answer prayer, and He speaks softly, in a manner that warms the heart.

Touched by the scene predicted for Jesus in this chapter, I was still crying. Then I heard the fulfillment of this prophecy in the New Testament, the manner in which he was crucified. There was no doubt about that being the fulfillment, for the details were astonishingly similar. I was glad I made a decision to be on Jesus' side rather than against him. Less than seven hours ago, I would have still said of the Jews' rebellion, "Good for them! I would have done the same."

I ached inside, again regretting my rebellion against the God of my forefathers. Then Paul Yates asked tenderly, "Would you like to know him as your Messiah now?" A fresh stream of tears poured out, obstructing my vision. I was unable to tell him of my private experience the previous night. I nodded yes, thinking perhaps there is a more "proper" way to do it.

Mr. Yates and I moved to a quieter section of the cabin, delaying breakfast. There, I had an urgent question before I consented to praying with him.

"Mr. Yates, would God be disappointed in me if I can't attend church?" I timidly asked. "I don't think my family would approve of that."

His wise reply to my question I will always remember. "God is not as interested in how much you go to church as in how much you love Him with your heart. If you desire to go to church, God can arrange it."

I was satisfied. He didn't push church-going, for he knew I was afraid to enter one. As we prayed quietly, I felt the same presence of God that I felt the night before, when I invited God's Son to be my friend and Savior. Last night's experience was more intense, and that was when I became a child of God. Praying with Mr. Yates merely reinforced my decision.

We reentered the kitchen for breakfast. After the meal, my decision was shared, although I felt this was a private matter between God and me. (This is a common Jewish feeling.) I found myself hugged and kissed by nearly everyone, and being welcomed into the "family of God."

Until this moment, I had not known the feeling of being loved. In my self-made prison no one could reach me. My prickly pear skin kept most people away. For the first time in my life, I let people love me -- I let them touch me! They were so happy for me that I was happy too. *Wait a minute... I... happy?* Unbelievably so. God was on my side, and I, on His.

*chapter eighteen*

# Family of God

**Though inundated by hugs** before leaving camp, I was yet incapable of reciprocating. Everyone participated in this excitement except one person. My mother stood off to the side query-eyed at the fuss that was made over me. I wondered why she ever bothered attending camp or Friday meetings. Though she seemed to enjoy socializing, without fail, five or so minutes into the message or Bible study she nodded off to sleep.

All the congratulations and hugs didn't impress me as much as being welcomed into the "family of God." That term became a longstanding comfort to me in the face of my shattered false hopes for a family life. Feeling like an orphan was not unique to my Israeli city life, nor to life in the orphanage. Even now at seventeen I felt parentless. Access to the Yateses was my only consolation. Now that I had, at last, made the long-awaited decision, my relationship with them grew even deeper. Friday meetings became my substitute for church.

Only two weeks after my camp conversion, I learned the true meaning of "family of God." A man-friend of my mother's came to visit one Saturday. He hadn't come around for some time, and noticed a new cabinet next to my mother's sewing machine. She explained it was my birthday gift to her a few months ago.

"How thoughtful," he turned to me. "How did you manage to have money for a cabinet?"

"I saved it up, for nearly a year, baby-sitting."

"Your ability for long-term planning is admirable," he said, and unwisely joked, "Who did you inherit this ability from, your mother or your father?"

"I don't know," I replied, not wanting to admit it could be from my mother.

An uneasy feeling came over me, and I wished he were through. *I* was. But he wouldn't leave it alone.

"You know, I'd really be interested in what kind of man your father is, so I can compare the chance I have with your mother."

Disgusted with his tactics, I told him that I didn't feel I needed to know about his interest in my mother and that I didn't appreciate him using me in order to win her. I wanted to make it obvious to him that I thought he didn't measure up to my father in any way.

"My father had plenty of good traits," I refused to specify.

"Your fadder vas crazy!" my mother suddenly yelled in her broken English.

Embarrassed, I stood my ground, feeling the need to defend Father's integrity.

In a rage, she turned over the cabinet I had given her, emptied its contents on the floor, picked up a drawer, and hurled it at me. I ducked. Then came another drawer, and the third as she screamed, "I don't vant your gift anymore, you alvays been curse to me. God punish me ven I conceive you, and curse me ven you born!"

Pierced to the core, my mind raced with questions. *A punishment and a curse? What was she guilty of?*

Right before her friend, she launched over toward me, grabbed my waist-long dark hair at the nape, and pulled so hard the pain immobilized me. She was considerably stronger than I, and as much as I struggled, I ended up lying on the floor. The last thing I remembered was seeing her leather-shoed foot out of the corner of my eye coming toward my head.

When I came to, I felt disoriented and had a splitting headache. I pulled myself onto the couch that was next to me. Realizing I was alone, I tried to recall the fight, unable to piece it together clearly for a while. Then my mother's raging insults about my being a curse to her superseded all the particulars. Thinking harder, I now recalled screaming back as I struggled helplessly, "This is the last time you will touch me!"

"Yes," I mumbled. "No more." I picked up the receiver of the phone that sat on the coffee table and dialed for Paul Yates.

"Can you please get me out of here, Mr. Yates," I cried. "She kicked me... in the head... and left."

Within ten minutes his car was waiting for me. I had already packed some clothes and toiletries. As I grabbed my bags, it occurred to me that the sun was going down, and that the incident occurred late morning. *How long had I been lying on the floor, alone?*

I had no trouble convincing Mr. Yates that I was unsafe with my mother. Emotionally, she had just caused irreparable damage to our already strained relationship. We talked all evening, he, Elizabeth, and I, though I was still shaky from the incident, and beginning to feel sick.

"Stay here for a couple of days," they offered their living room couch.

*Just a couple of days?* I thought, and then tearfully declared, "I can't ever go back to live with her..."

"We don't want you to return to your mother," they surprised me. "But we don't have an extra bedroom to keep you," said Elizabeth.

"I don't take much space," I pleaded.

Now Paul, misty-eyed, explained, "Sweetheart," he called me as usual, "if there were a way, we would adopt you, but it would be a complicated legal procedure. Besides, you are seventeen, ready to be on your own."

I didn't feel I was ready, but I wasn't feeling well enough to protest.

"We are praying for another way," said Paul. "Let me make some phone calls in the morning to make some arrangements."

*I am forever a victim of arrangements,* I thought, but still felt privileged that adoption even occurred to them. Paul and Elizabeth Yates, already in their fifties, were childless. I realized having me in their home would disrupt their lives, and make ministry more difficult. The thought of someone caring that much was comforting enough.

Two days later Mr. Yates drove me to an older Christian

couple's home. He had explained my situation to them over the phone. Mr. and Mrs. Loux' children were married and gone. Our "arrangement" was unique. The Yateses had contacted the head of *Friends of Israel,* a friend of Paul since Poland. I was to receive a scholarship sum of seventy-five dollars per month. From these funds I was to pay fifty dollars for my room and board. The rest I could use for myself. As long as I attended college and maintained reasonable grades, the funds would continue. The Louxes were delighted. They had been praying about boarding foreign students, and this marked the beginning of their ministry.

They treated me as if I were their daughter, and, as God would have it, took me to church regularly. Meanwhile, my mother and I did not speak with each other. Apparently, Paul Yates went to see her to explain that we were both better off with this arrangement. She never protested, nor did she ever ask me why I decided to leave.

In the fall I started college, majoring in linguistics with French as one of my languages. Once settled into a routine, and getting used to my new life, I decided to call Mischa on the phone to tell him of my experience with God. My voice was untypically enthusiastic. When I was finished, there was a short silence, and then Mischa's serious, slow voice broke in.

"I think, Yaffa, that you will get over this. You are a teenager in need of something to hold on to. This is just a passing fancy. There is no way it will stick. You are a Jew!"

"Yes, Mischa, a completed Jew."

"No, a desperate one. It's probably our fault."

"Is that why you are an atheist?"

"I am an atheist because I think religion is a crutch, for people who are too weak to face death. Heaven is a figment of their imagination, and God is only a wish to ease their pain."

"Then how is my conversion your and the family's fault?"

"We never gave you a taste of Judaism. We never even took you to a synagogue. With your personality, religion is helpful, but you should, at least, accept Judaism."

"I do, and then some."

"Listen, Yaffa, next week is Yom Kippur (Day of Atonement), you know how I feel about religion and synagogues and all..." he hesitated. "If I go to Temple service, would *you* go?" This was a challenge not an appeal.

"Sure, I'll go."

"You're on!"

For the first time I entered a synagogue for a service. Mischa and I were, no doubt, the only Israelis there. We were separated, the men on the first floor, the women on the second. Reading the Hebrew prayers, which were mispronounced all around me, I realized that no one prayed any prayer accept the assigned ones. How cheated I felt! Halfway through the service I could no longer contain myself, as some Jews were in tears reading the prayers of the patriarchs in order to entreat God to forgive their sins. I too burst into tears, for them. *My God, how much I appreciate your salvation and forgiveness once and for all!* As people dispersed from the synagogue, I felt a stranger among them, though they were my own kind. Mischa and I never discussed the service.

Once when I was visiting Mischa and his family several years later, he nearly threw me out of the house. He was angry when he realized my beliefs were not a passing fancy.

I wrote a letter to Father, telling him that I now hear from God. An angry reply came promptly, "Don't claim that God talks to you. It's obvious he doesn't. He did so only with the prophets." Then I received an even angrier letter from Aunt Marga, forbidding me to write to Father about my "distorted Christian views." Aunt Marga, an atheist herself, and now in speaking terms with Father again, was "protecting" him from my "outrageous" claims. As far as she was concerned, Father couldn't think for himself. I differed with her on that.

"Dear Marga," I replied. "Abba must have a chance to prove that he can be a useful person. Please help him by encouraging him to continue painting and drawing. That is what he needs." I'd been praying for Father's freedom.

Soon Father wrote to me with joy. "I have my own studio, and I am no longer institutionalized." Occasionally, he sent me a formal invitation to one of his art exhibits. *If he can work for a living*, I thought, *he can think for himself, and, yes hold an argument about God without falling apart mentally.* But my hands were tied. After telling him that I had prayed for his freedom from the institution, he stopped writing for some time.

I now came to an overwhelming realization -- an awakening -- that my true family is the family of God. Not only did I feel closer to Christians than to Jews, but also to Christians compared with my family of flesh and blood. How God compensates!

Almost immediately after I was settled at the Louxes'

home, Paul Yates snatched me away nearly every Sunday evening and often week nights. He took me to different churches, not for me to attend, but for me to give my testimony. We traveled throughout the county, wherever Mr. Yates booked me. He had me speak in nearly every evangelical church within about a one hundred mile radius. I did this mainly out of gratefulness for his patient, loving concern since that first day I met him.

"You see, I have an investment in you," I remembered. Soon after the first time he stated this, I carried this thought in my heart, despite my rebellion. Several times he used this statement as an analogy for me to understand what an investment God had in me through Jesus. Once I understood the spiritual meaning of this statement, I realized why he chose this to be one of his first challenges to me. Now I felt obliged to return the investment.

Paul Yates knew I was terrified to speak before these congregations, and he reminded me of the countless times I sang Hebrew songs at his informal gatherings. I fondly remembered how he always bragged me up. And now, without explaining how to give a testimony, he said, "Bring your tambourine, sing some Hebrew songs, and tell them what's on your heart."

That is precisely what I did. After two songs, I merely told a short version of my life, bringing most of the women, and even some men to tears. Then I started walking away from the pulpit, finished as far as I was concerned. Suddenly I darted back to the microphone with an afterthought, "uh... and then I accepted Jesus as my Messiah," and left the podium. I had done this several times, having spoken for an hour or so at a time, before Mr. Yates hinted that it might help to include God before the very last sentence of my testimony.

Amazingly, no one ever commented on my non-testimonial testimony. Instead, countless people in various churches, touched to the core, came up to me in tears, telling how this increased their love for the Jews. God saw fit to use even my unprofessional, pity-drawing story.

For two years, I spoke more than I sat in a pew. It was good for me, for I began to understand that true Christians love the Jews. What a warm feeling that was! No more persecution. No more Jewish pride for survival.

*chapter nineteen*

# *First Lessons from God*

**One day I received a phone call** at the Loux residence. Three people, preparing for ministry to Israel, wanted to study Hebrew from an Israeli Christian. Would I consider teaching them once a week, inquired the spokesman.

"I would have to interview the three of you before taking on the task of teaching you to witness to Jews, especially in Israel," I said, testingly.  .

"Can we meet right away?" insisted the voice.

Contemplating for a moment, I made a decision.

"Meet me at 1248 Hillview Avenue, in twenty minutes."

That was my mother's address. I thought this a way for me to renew communications without being alone with her. To conduct the interview in her apartment would serve more than one purpose. I quickly called her for the first time in eight months.

When I arrived, two men and a woman already sat in my mother's living room, the scene of my blackout.

My mother didn't hear me letting myself in. She was stirring some dishes in the kitchen. That is what she always did when nervous around people.

The interview was well in progress when my mother, obviously having overheard it all, burst into the living room and apologized for interrupting. I thought she was going to talk to me.

"Please, don't mind me to ask," she addressed my interviewees with all the charm she had. She got the attention -- even mine. "Vhy you vant to learn Hebrew? You are Christians."

"Because we love the Jews," came an instant reply.

I smiled in agreement.

"I don't understand. You are gentiles. Vat you do viz Hebrew?"

"We want to understand the Bible and its people better, and to speak to them."

"You go to make more Christians from Jew peoples?"

"Not make them Christians, but bring them to *their* Jewish Messiah. When Jesus filled us with himself, he also filled us with love for his people, like you. Our hearts are burning inside to show them how much God loves them."

My mother stepped backward and nearly tripped. She then shook her head in dismay and retreated into the kitchen. She said not a word to me.

The results of the interview were satisfying. First of all, I needed to see how these people responded to an unbelieving Jew, such as my mother. They passed my test. Few people can handle "prickly pears." Secondly, I wanted my mother to receive a dose of true Christianity which recognizes and loves its Jewish roots, the likes of which she had never seen.

Thirdly, seeing that she was not yet open to communication with me was the only disappointment.

I taught my students at one of their homes and discovered that these three represented the desires and attitudes of most of their church members. Soon I was invited to give my testimony there.

Never before had I been personally asked to give my testimony. Always Mr. Yates had me booked. I agreed, making this my first independent venture for God.

Strangely, it never occurred to me to find out what denomination the church was. To me, Christians believed in my friend Jesus, and that was good enough.

When I arrived for the evening service, there was a Jewish high school teacher whom I knew from the Yates' meetings. He too was to give his testimony. This service was "Jewish night."

Neither of us knew what we were in for, nor were we aware that the church had been praying for us to receive the baptism in the Holy Spirit, and anticipated results.

I hadn't so much as heard of such a thing. Holy Ghost? That sounded like a joke or a curse word. *No ghost for me, thank you!*

After my testimony I sat on the front pew. The pastor invited the congregation to pray, to end the service, I thought. Prayer for the nation of Israel bombarded Heaven.

I was sitting with very "proper" prayer posture when some rustling and moving around prompted me to open my eyes. To my amazement, several people were on their knees turned around in their pews, the rest stood with arms lifted up. My first instinct was to think them unduly irreverent. Then, I realized some of their prayer words were not in

English. What's more, I wondered at people's unusual movements.

I asked God, "What is going on, is this all right, or had I walked into something other than Christian?" God instantly responded, and I was suddenly reminded of Abraham and Moses, and as I watched these people, God was saying to me: "Look! These people worship me as your forefathers did. Don't be afraid." Then I also remembered that many Jews pray while swaying back and forth. Suddenly, I felt at home with this kind of worship. Yet I was still sitting, proper and stiff in my pew.

I appreciated gentiles worshiping like Jews, but I never thought that God wanted *me* to do the same. Till now, I had been willing to accept whatever Christian practices dictated. I thought I gave up Jewish ways. So, even though I was impressed, I argued with God that I didn't need this, all the while being the only one still in my seat.

It was in the midst of my arguing and protesting that I found myself on my knees, telling God that I now wanted everything He had for me. The transition between sitting and kneeling, I cannot remember. During that time, about thirty or so people gathered around me, fervently praying for my baptism of the Spirit.

No one had explained to me what it was, or why different languages were involved. So with my Jewish thinking, I bargained with God: *O.K. Lord, I speak many languages. That is not a phenomenon for me. But I do not recognize the languages spoken here. They don't seem to be of this world. Lord, you know that I never learned how to praise you in the languages which I speak. If you will supernaturally allow me to speak words of worship in these earthly languages, I will know that this is of you.*

As I prayed, minding my own business, several people began to tug forcefully at my arms, loudly commanding me to do and say specific things. All I wished to do was to be with God, to do and say what *He* was already tenderly telling me. What people insisted upon doing to me clashed with what God was doing within me. Had I not been deeply desiring to follow God, I would have cancelled the entire affair. But I was now convinced. God was giving me those words of worship in the six languages, and I tried to ignore man's formulas. The Holy Spirit was, at the same time showing me that God is individual, and He works uniquely with each person, according to His discretion.

"Please, Lord, let me have some peace and privacy with you," I entreated in my heart.

In a moment, everyone around moved away and my aching arms returned to me. Most left for home, and some remained to quietly pray with the pastor. At last, three hours later, having been left alone, I received my heavenly language.

Next week, zealously, I went to my pastor to tell him the good news. He patiently listened me out. I told him every detail. Then he began to speak with great concern.

"What you need is water baptism, as was done by John the Baptist in the gospels. What you told me about is not for today," he warned.

"Then how could it have happened to me?" I challenged.

"Please come back for counseling. This sort of thing is dangerous and we must help you let it go," he instructed.

Shocked and disappointed, I thanked him for his time and never returned for counseling. I had just enough confidence in God to realize that my pastor did not understand, and it was obvious to me that he was afraid of what I shared with him.

On the subject of water baptism, however, I had heard from a friend that some Christians believe in sprinkling rather than immersing. My friend was very persistent in trying to convince me of her denomination's point of view. As a result, I delayed my decision to be water-baptized until I developed my own conviction on this matter.

In college, I now had the desire to carry my Bible at the top of my book pile. This was in the mid-sixties, when boys and girls alike began wearing long hair and one couldn't tell them apart. They wore ragged clothes, claiming, "God is dead." It was also the critical period when prayer had just been taken out of schools. "Religion" was taboo and philosophy and promiscuity were lauded.

Inevitably, as I was hoping, someone would confront me in the hallway, cafeteria or outside saying, "D'you really believe what's in this book?" pointing to my Bible.

"Sure do!" I responded, and a chance to witness would follow. I became known on campus for carrying my Bible. Often several tall boys would surround me. At four-feet ten inches, that was uncomfortable. They sometimes plotted and got together to contest my beliefs. God always gave me words to say, and they left being challenged instead of being the challengers.

It was time to be baptized. One Sunday, the pastor drove this home in a touching sermon. As hard as it was for me to do anything publicly, I knew I had to do it. Now I had to make my decision -- will it be immersion in this church, or sprinkling in another church? Unfortunately, whichever method I chose would mark me as a denominationalist, something I dreaded. *I am a child of God; I belong to the family of God, not to a denomination.*

Returning home, I opened my Hebrew New Testament that Mr. Yates had given me. Reading and rereading the passages about John the Baptist, I suddenly broke out laughing. The full implication of the name "John the Baptist" became clear to me. In the Hebrew, I read (translated) "John the dunker."

*If the method of John the "dunker" was right for Jesus, it is right for me,* I concluded.

The next Sunday evening, friends from another church came to watch the baptismal service. I was last in line of six candidates. Nervously, I rehearsed in my mind the procedure drilled in baptismal class. One after another we were very quickly "dunked." When I arose from the water, the first breath I inhaled was more than air. It felt as if I had breathed in the very presence of God: I wanted to cry and laugh at the same time. I stood behind the now closed curtain dripping on the plush new carpet, eyes closed. Abruptly, and rudely I felt, I was tapped on the shoulder and reminded to hurry to the changing room. My long hair still damp, I sat down next to my friends. Misty-eyed, I felt like I was about to burst. This was in the middle of the closing hymn. One of my friends, the one who believed in sprinkling, turned to me and whispered, "Why are you crying, do you regret being immersed?"

"Regret? No! I feel like someone just corked my throat... I want to praise God, but its improper here."

She shrugged her shoulders and very properly joined in the last stanza of the hymn, while I sobbed. How disappointed I felt that there was no time allotted within all the calloused tradition to give thanks to God for the miracle that baptism represents. Visualizing Jesus being baptized in water and in the Spirit at once, I pondered, *Who rushed Him out of the water?*

In college, I had been all this time associating mainly with foreign-born students. Our college had the largest "International" club in northern California, with more than two hundred members. Being around various nationalities was for me like being at home.

Once, in the cafeteria, my ears perked up when I heard Arabic spoken at a table three rows from me. After awhile I walked over to the two Arabs and greeted them in Arabic, feeling like I had found someone almost akin to me. They greeted me back asking a few questions. As soon as I said I was an Israeli, they started ignoring me. I knew then that I was no longer welcome to speak to them. The American melting pot was quite frozen in this case.

During my second year at college, I was running for the vice presidency of the huge International Club. I had been well accepted by everyone there, and was confident that I would win over the other two candidates. Election day was next morning. Candidates had already turned in their forms to the dean's office for approval. I was eating my lunch in the cafeteria when Bill, a tall senior and acting president of the crumbling Christian Club approached me. I had attended Christian Club twice, at the expense of missing International Club meetings, so never returned.

"Yaffa, I've been praying," he told me as he sat down. "I really feel you should run for president of Christian Club."

"You're joking."

"No."

"Why the last minute?"

"I couldn't find you, and wanted to have peace about the matter. You know how God usually acts at the last possible moment."

I didn't, yet.

"It's impossible, Bill, I'm already running for another club."

"I know. That's why I prayed so long. It made no sense to me, but I am sure you are the one."

"Why me, anyway? No one other than you even knows me there."

"Wait till I tell you who's running against you," he teased.

"Against me? I thought I would be taking your place? Who is it?"

"Ron."

"Everyone knows him! I have no chance. Besides, he's a boy. Girls don't get elected by Christians. I'm sorry, I'm already committed. They need me at International."

"God needs you at Christian."

Bill stood up and said, "Pray about it, Yaffa, and if you feel to do it, go to the office within the hour. I know it's past deadline, but God is able." He left.

I was in a quandary. How could I leave International? I had never been without foreigners around me... not even in Israel. I was angered that Bill would confront me so late, knowing the odds were against me. *How arrogant of him to expect me to switch loyalties,* I thought.

This was my first lesson in consciously seeking God's will

on a matter. I decided to pray, right there in the bustling cafeteria. Again, I made a deal with God. "There are three of us running for vice president, Lord. If you want me to run for Christian Club, then make it a three-way tie. Then I'll know it's you. But, if you do it this way, I won't be able switch club candidacy until after International's election. How am I going to make it in time for the other election, Lord?"

The decision was agonizing. I felt I was about to be uprooted and transplanted into unfamiliar territory. "I don't know how to be a Christian Club president, Lord," I complained.

Next morning, tense with uncertainty and with prayers under my breath, I entered International Club. As I seated myself to cast my votes, I decided to vote for one of my opponents, rather than for myself. I kept watching the clock. It was twenty minutes past the hour. My tense body could scarcely stay seated. Votes were finally tallied, first for secretary, then for treasurer...

*Well, Lord, this is either your doing or my foolishness,* I prayed. The Club president looked at the tallies and shook his head. "Here, count them again, he ordered his vice president." The clock showed 9:25. I was getting sick with anxiety.

9:32, and still counting. The vice president completed his count and whispered something to the president. "We have to have a tie-breaker for the office of vice president," announced the baffled president. "All three candidates had an equal number of votes."

"Ehm," I cleared my throat and raised a shaky hand. "I would like to take this opportunity to decline, and let the tie be broken between the other two candidates. I'm sorry to have to do this, but I am needed elsewhere." I rushed out of the room, feeling like a traitor.

I must have looked like a maniac running down the length of the corridor to the farthest end of the campus. "This is really crazy, Lord," I muttered between breaths. "They won't accept a new candidate *during* an election. Christian club is probably done voting anyway."

The office door was open, and the secretary watched me bursting in. I glanced at the clock: 9:47.

"What are you in such a hurry for?" she barked.

*Perfect opening, thank you, Lord!* I didn't know how to ask for such a crazy change.

"I am in a hurry because I think I am missing my own election," I started, breathlessly.

"What?" she asked, puzzled.

"I don't have time to explain, but I have an urgent request. Please change my candidacy from that of vice president of International Club to that of president of Christian Club, quick!"

"My, we're coming up in the world, aren't we?" she mocked. She then glanced at the clock, and asked, "Are you serious?"

I nodded, impatiently but solemnly, watching the clock hit 9:50. She sighed disapprovingly, scratched her signature on a form, and said, "I hope their clock isn't fast, good luck!"

As I rushed back to the other end of the campus, my heart was beating violently, not so much from running but from excitement. As insane as this seemed, I suddenly felt released, free to do the right thing in God's eyes. Half the miracle was over; I was relieved.

"It's up to you, Lord," I told God, as I reached for the door knob of Christian Club. I gulped a deep breath and opened the door.

"Hello Yaffa, just in time for congratulations!" declared Bill. On the board, the tallies showed I won by an overwhelming majority! I plunged myself into a seat, exhausted, marveling at the completion of God's miracle.

The crumbling club of a mere seven members somehow grew to twenty-three, then to more than fifty that year. I was forced to search and study the Scriptures for Bible study preparation. Still more comfortable in the Hebrew language, I tended to express my thoughts as I remembered them in Hebrew or as I thought they might be better understood with the Hebraic mind set. Hoping to be able to translate directly from the Hebrew, I expressed my wish for a complete Hebrew Bible of the Old and New Testaments.

At the end of a club Bible study one day, the members all shouted, "Happy nineteenth birthday!" They then presented me with a gift-wrapped package. It contained the Hebrew Bible they had ordered six weeks before, all the way from New York. A spokesman said, "From now on, teach us from the Hebrew."

Every break, I devoured my Hebrew Bible. I began comparing it to different English versions. Though it helped to read more than one version, I was disappointed that the richness of the Hebrew was somehow lost. As a linguist, I wanted to bring out what I felt had been lost. I translated a verse here, a passage there, sharing tidbits of translation with not only the members of the Christian Club but with my young-adult Sunday school teacher in my new church.

She urged me to teach some of it to our class. How hungry many of the gentile Christians were to see Scripture in its original context!

For years to come, wherever I attended church, I would end up doing Hebrew word studies, speaking before various groups and often helping pastors with Hebrew words for sermons. I came to realize that my interest in linguistics was to be used for God's purposes and not for the United Nations, or some other career.

Toward the end of my second year in college I decided to move from Oakland, in northern California, to Los Angeles, scarcely letting anyone know about it. After all, I rationalized, who really cares where I am? And there is no one to hold me here. With a quick, cold telephone call I shocked my mother.

"What about finishing college?" she asked.

"What I want to learn I cannot get in college. I am joining a ministry."

"That's crazy! You don't know anyone in Los Angeles."

"I have known the people I'm going with... uh... for two days now." I could almost hear her shaking her head. "Gotta go -- they are waiting," I said, and hung up with an unregretful goodby.

I did join this ministry for a while, living on my own for the first time. I thought of the comment that Mr. Yates had made after I left my mother's home, "You are ready to go on your own." Now, two years later, I *was* ready. To be ready to live on my own was one thing, but to make major decisions without advice was another.

Left to my own devices, I married three months after meeting a young man just out of the marines. After six years, and three children, we all moved to northern California. I was glad to be back. Even now, as wife and mother, I was invited to speak on occasion, mostly to share my testimony.

*chapter twenty*

# Second Discovery

**A woman came to me** a week after she had heard my testimony, saying, "I have been praying for you ever since the meeting. I can't shake the feeling that you should write your story for a book."

That thought had occurred to me before but I refused, not wanting to get emotionally involved with my past. "Speaking makes me nervous enough," I explained. "Writing a biography takes intense involvement." The woman looked disappointed, so I promised to take the matter up with God, and so the task began.

Halfway into writing the book, I came to a dead end. I realized that I had serious doubts about myself and my parents. After months of writing I questioned whether I would ever be able to sort out the whole truth. I'd been struggling with some missing links since before age eight. Conflicting versions I had accumulated throughout my childhood left me wondering. *Who am I really? Who dare I ask?*

Father? He is still unable to cope with painful questions about our past. What's more, Aunt Marga had long forbidden my stirring up of Holocaust memories in my letters for fear of another emotional breakdown. Soliciting his help was out of the question.

Aunt Marga? For many years we haven't corresponded. Even so, we have never communicated on this level.

Mischa? He is unlikely to know firsthand the details I am after.

"I have no one to turn to for reliable information, Lord," I complained. "How can I complete my story? The only other family member who survived the Holocaust is my mother..."

*"Her? Lord, you want me to ask her?"*

I procrastinated, wallowing in reawakened desire to find out the truth. Once again I groped for my identity. I desperately needed to know specific facts about my background, more for my emotional well-being than for the book.

Resolving my lifelong questions appeared hopeless unless I confronted my mother. How I dreaded this task! I would spend most of my time sorting out what I didn't believe. Months passed as I contemplated the visit and what I would ask her.

The opportunity unexpectedly presented itself for me and my children to visit *Savta*, Hebrew for "grandmother." I alone knew the true mission of this visit. Prepared for "war," I armed myself with a list of questions, pencil, and paper.

The visit was emotionally draining, as always, in her small

cluttered apartment with little space to move. Evading her judgmental third-degree, right down to what kind of meals I'd been cooking, was another stress. As yet, no opportunity presented itself for my interview with her, and we decided to return home.

"Please stay overnight," begged my mother.

My first reaction to her request was the usual unyielding refusal. After a tense exchange of beseeching and excuses between us, I relented. I wasn't sure whether the victory was hers or mine.

"Imma, I am writing a book on my life and I need some information about our background," I managed awkwardly, after awhile.

She thought for a moment, as if to consider her options.

"If you writing 'bout yourself, vy you digging so far back?" she countered.

"Because it's all part of me," I explained. "You," I struggled to confess, "are also part of... my background."

"Vid all I vent trough," she whined, "I could write a book myself."

*Sure she could,* I thought, *and hash over the same old sob story. Can't she just tell the truth?*

"Sure I help you," she surprised me, "Vat you vant to know?"

*Brave of her. Doesn't she realize her integrity is at stake?*

"I know much of what happened, Imma," I assured her. "You don't need to repeat all you've told us for years, every time you visited us outside of Abba's house in Israel. Then, when Mischa and I came to America, you told it to us again and again. If you just answer my questions, that will help me."

*"Lord, spare me the agony of hearing it all again,"* I begged.

She *did* repeat it -- the same old sob story. Nothing in it changed. Always, Mischa and I had reacted to it by screaming for her to stop bringing up the past, for we knew her version conflicted with "ours."

I constrained myself to listen without showing antagonism. Yet I judged her every facial expression and tested the tones of her voice, searching for evidence of lying or truthfulness. It was still difficult to believe her claims of heroism before, during, and after the holocaust.

*If she was such a heroine, why did she abandon me before I was three?* I reasoned resentfully, as she paused.

I decided to pose this most urgent question. It would be the ultimate test of her honesty and true feelings toward me as her child.

Diplomatically, I took the floor. "I remember once when I was still in diapers... waking up..." I searched for tactful, non-offensive words. "I cried and cried for a long time. Did you, I mean... What happened?"

Her face contorted with pain. She bent her standing body toward me, and shouted her desperate Hungarian protest.

"It was a setup! A cruel and ugly setup!" Her body shook with anger as she recounted her version of the abandonment. "Your grandmother had to make me look guilty. In the pioneering years in Israel, rabbinical laws did not permit divorce except for unfaithfulness or child abandonment."

Now she shook an angry fist in the air and switched to English, "Your grandmodder, she never care for me, even in Hungary. It vas her idea. She push and push and push your fadder until..."

A silent outburst of emotion overwhelmed me as she repeated the same divorce story that she had told for so many years without any change. *How could she do that if it were a lie? Would she react so strongly to the subject?*

*"Dear Lord,"* I breathed a prayer, *"the conflict has not been between her and me. She had been given no chance to tell her side of the story, and so directed her bitterness at me, the easiest target. It hardly matters now whether she really abandoned me or whether it was a setup. Perhaps both sides have some truth -- I shall never know. What matters is that I am not angry with her anymore. If she had been wronged this much, I feel for her."*

An unfamiliar feeling surged through me and with it I found myself letting go of past prejudices, opinions and emotional obstacles. Twenty-seven years of hatred painfully passed before me. *Lord, please forgive me,* I silently pleaded.

In one moment, my lifelong inner struggle over my mother's genuineness came to an end, her words no longer falling on deaf ears. Now, with the overwhelming experience of a complete emotional turnabout, at last, I felt she was my mother regardless of her faults. I sensed that her need for me to believe her was at least as intense as my own need to be wanted by her.

I whispered an inaudible sigh. Unwelcome moisture stubbornly welled up in my eyes when I finally realized that unfamiliar feeling was a tinge of love -- something I never felt for her. Yet I said nothing. She was in no condition to understand.

I was still sitting on the green dining room chair. Mother was standing in the narrow kitchen a few feet from me. Somehow, she looked different, frail and vulnerable. It never occurred to me that she could be this way. I almost pitied her.

Oblivious to my emotional turmoil and change of heart, she was unburdening. How could I have been so heartless all these years?

"Tell me about our escape to Israel," I entreated.

Nodding "yes," her eyes searched my paper. "You been writing English or Hungarian?" she quizzed.

I hadn't been writing. She never noticed. As if it mattered, I assured her that I could do it in either language. She chose to tell the story in Hungarian, I chose to write it in English. We both prepared ourselves for the task, she by setting down some dishes, I by sitting tall and setting pencil to paper. Nervously, I awaited the rest of the mysterious missing information.

"I and Abba, and your brother set out from Budapest, Hungary to begin our journey to Palestine in early 1939," Mother began.

*Early 1939? Seven and a half years before my birth? This could not be the same escape of which I knew.*

"We escaped, illegally, by train from Hungary. Our intentions were to settle and build a Jewish homeland..."

I knew my parents were pioneers to Israel, but underestimated their fervor.

"The escape was promoted by the Zionist movement in Europe." She bent toward me and placed a forefinger on her lips. Wide-eyed and playing it up in her charming English, she whispered, "Vas all done unde'ground... you know... ve-e-ry dengerous.''

After a while, I interrupted her, "My name... Why did you name me Yaffa? Such a modern Hebrew name. You speak Hungarian, not Hebrew.''

"What!" she shouted with indignation. "Did you think we knew nothing? Your father and I were involved in the Zionist movement for years. Even as teenagers we trained children to become pioneers for Palestine. We needed to know no Hebrew, but we had access to Hebrew names. All that I have told you took place before the war. Then we decided to get married, since both of us wanted to go to Israel.''

For the first time a dim flicker of a spark showed in her eyes and her voice became proud.

*Zionist movement? Were my parents involved in Zionism? Why had I never been told that?* Somehow, it was difficult to picture my parents as activists of any kind. I only knew them to be sad -- desperately sad -- lacking ambition, bitter, and utterly tired of life. Zionists who accomplished anything were tenacious, fearlessly risking their lives.

"For two years, we made plans and underground connections in Hungary,'' she continued as if she hadn't been interrupted. "When the war came we lost these connections.

"Caught by the Nazis en route to Palestine, we were deported to Germany. Our efforts to renew connections from there were unsuccessful. Your father became a political prisoner with a life sentence for his involvement in smuggling one hundred and sixty-one Jews out of Hungary to Palestine.

"The Russians bought your father from the Nazis after

two and a half years in prison. He was to paint the portraits of their leaders, but refused. For this, he was given a second life sentence and sent to a Siberian slave camp.'' Mother paused, and sadly said, ''I lost two cousins in Siberia,'' and continued. ''Ruthlessly worked and literally starved, they were all slaves. Those who survived the torture, cold, hunger, and brainwashing wished they hadn't. Your father was among them.''

*No wonder Father had emotional problems.*

''We had no choice but to wait out the war,'' Mother said, discounting the five years of torture and suffering caused by the Holocaust. ''If we could just stay alive, somehow, someday we knew we would make it to Palestine.''

''Your second escape,'' I blurted out. She nodded. I marveled at the striking contrast between ''the old sob story'' of torture, suffering, resentment and self-pity, and her last statement. They vowed to reach their future homeland. This was my only tell-tale sign that, indeed, she and Father were tenacious, and, yes, fearless back then. It was clear to me that neither war nor an inopportune pregnancy was going to stop them from reaching their goal. How much the war changed them!

Mother was unaware that I was nearly bursting emotionally. For the first time, I felt proud of them.

''You were born in a refugee camp, called U.N.R.A. (United Nations Refugee Aid), in Germany occupied Bavaria. The camp was made up of long wooden barracks, like a military station, with about twenty rooms each and only two bathrooms and one small kitchen.

''Though free to go in and out of camp, we had nothing,

for our possessions were long before confiscated by the Nazis. Though the war was over, we were still persecuted. Your father and I lost our home shortly after we were married..." Mother paused for a sorrowful sigh, then continued with obvious effort to cover up the emotional pain she was feeling. I felt it. For the first time I felt the pain with her, though I, too, concealed it.

"I was working as cook for the Russian troop stationed near the camp in exchange for food when I was pregnant with you. Food was scarce. One morning I was ordered to cook some horse meat which I found to be spoiled. I insisted that it should not be cooked. The captain ordered me to cook it anyway. Then I was ordered to be the first one to eat of it. Soon, I started doubling over with cramps. He found me slouched against the kitchen wall.

"The captain marched me three miles to the hospital to receive treatment. I was diagnosed to have highly contagious typhoid. Fearful of an epidemic and unwilling to treat a Jewess at the hospital, a doctor prescribed an herbal tea and sent me on my way. The tea saved my life and yours."

*"Lord, your hand was in this, wasn't it?"*

"I had just barely recovered from the typhoid and was very weak when I went into labor while cooking. The captain must have felt guilty that he had caused me so much trouble. He marched me again the three miles to the German hospital, this time in the deep December snow. The captain and I both expected that they would refuse to deliver a Jewish baby."

"Where was Abba all this time?" I seized the opportunity.

"He was making new connections, secretly," she replied and then went on. "The labor was intensely difficult. When you finally appeared, you weighed a mere four pounds, so tiny, you lay in the doctor's big hand."

"I knew that, Imma, you told me once," I announced with a big smile.

She chuckled with a twinkle in her eye, "I never told you how I was admitted into the hospital."

"Didn't they refuse you again?"

"No," she broke out laughing. "You were born under the point of the Russian captain's gun, aimed at the Nazi doctor's head!"

"I guess the German doctor got persuaded," I joked in English.

"Yes, but he vas very hard on me," she answered, dead serious again, and excused herself to dry her eyes.

At this point, I recalled knowing that Mother's illness caused her to be dry of breast milk, and me, near death. A German woman who gave birth the same day in that hospital took pity on us. She nursed me along with her own infant until I gained a fighting chance. Years later, I met my German "wet-nurse" in Israel. She and her Jewish husband immigrated there when I was about nine years old. I was invited to spend many pleasant days with her and her family.

"It was still snowing outside," Mother regained composure, "when I and your Abba brought you from the hospital to camp."

"We had no panes in the windows, because they had been bombed out. We had neither heat nor hot water. Constant hunger was our lot. After you were born, I traded the cigarettes from the U.N.'s aid packages for food for us and for canned milk for you. I also kept your ungrateful grandmother alive.''

*Perhaps she did,* I thought, though Grandmother always claimed the reverse.

"What happened next?" I urged her on to keep her thoughts off Grandmother.

"Before you were born, I sewed an inside pocket in my wide coat, large enough to hide you in it. One day, a group from the Zionist movement showed up at camp. They quickly drew up a random list of those who should leave for Palestine. We had been waiting for this.

"In the darkness of the night we started in truck loads to France. There we were crowded into what we were told to be only a temporary camp, meant for a day or two. It was worse than in Germany. News came to us that another ship, three months before, was captured by the English near Palestine. Consequently, we remained there for a long time, until it was safe to meet the next connection.

"Somewhere near Marseille, about half a mile from the port, our boat awaited in the open water. Clad in worn out clothes and shoes, carrying children whose mouths were taped, we waded in the ice-cold water to reach the boat. This was an unexpected inconvenience.''

*What patience and perseverance they must have possessed.*

"Imma, I have been told that we landed in Cypress before we could enter Palestine. How were we treated there?"

"We had been sailing for thirteen days, nearing destination, when the English surrounded and captured our boat in the same manner that they did the one before us.

The British had not yet given up their military base in Palestine, and allowed no Jews to enter. Instead, they transported us to Cypress. There, the heat was unbearable for us Europeans, as was the ever presence of the cold, cruel two-legged British watchdogs, who kept us from escaping."

"Imma, what about when the English released us?" I asked anxiously, as this was another of my "fragments."

"After a wait of some months, everyone's health was failing. Infants were dying from the heat, unsanitary conditions, and hunger. This being after the war, it became a political embarrassment to the British. Finally, they decided to ship a quota of families, only those who had infants, to Palestine. Since you were under a year, we were part of that transport. I do not know what happened to the rest."

*"Lord, your hand was in every instance to save my life, wasn't it?"* I thanked Him, and realized that I was the cause of their chance to enter the Promised Land. I wondered if anyone appreciates this small but significant fact. In this instance I saw myself as a blessing, not a curse.

"How did you feel, I mean, how was life in Israel at this time? I know it was no bed of roses, but can you give me some details?" I asked, hoping to capture the pioneering spirit.

"Of course, life wasn't easy," she replied reluctantly. "Since your father had no work, and we lived in a wooded shack. After a period of quarantine for health purposes, we stayed in a dirty, smelly, partially bombed Arab house with no proper facilities..."

Clearly she didn't care to talk about it. Only the sad and the bad remained important to her. I changed the subject as

I followed her through the hallway to the linen closet with pad in hand. Getting some bedding for me, she headed for the living room couch, I tailing behind like a reporter. The children were finally asleep.

Now it was I who was emotionally involved; Mother was ready to end the ordeal.

"Do you remember the first Independence Day, when Palestine became Israel in 1948?" I asked, again hoping to spark some positive emotions.

"Yes, I r'member," she switched to her broken English in response to my English question. "Big celebrash'n... our family vatch from de rooftop," she spoke in monotone voice, flicking a hand in the air as a non-caring gesture. "Ve 'rived in 1947, you know, before all dat." At this she decided to go brush her teeth.

*How could this subject be without meaning to her?* I wondered, greatly disappointed in her matter-of-factness.

*How much she must have changed,* I thought, with a piercing heartache of my own. I wished to have known my real mother, the mother who claimed she hid me in an inside coat pocket. How much she must have suffered, as she has been trying to tell me all these years. She cannot even recount the most joyful event in Jewish history, Israel's first Independence Day! That triumphant day, which fulfilled a two-thousand-year-old hope, she described with no feeling -- an empty voice. I bled for her, an emotion I had never felt toward Mother. I smiled at her when she returned, having no words to describe what was taking place in my heart that night.

In my blind hatred of her, I had been oblivious of her desperate attempts to marry someone willing and financially

187

able to take us in. Now I recall two of those marriages, ending in divorce. Regardless of whether the custody judgment was based on truth or falsehood, I can now see she was genuinely longing to gain me back. The puzzle was nearly finished, and I was finally, though painfully late, at age thirty, my mother's daughter.

"Imma," I called, my voice quivering and my hands perspiring.

"Vat, dear?"

"Imma," I repeated with feeling. "You know," I choked, "some of your story was hard for me to believe... well," I paused to choose my words kindly, "but you understand why, don't you? I mean... it wasn't my fault."

She barely nodded her head.

The intensity and implication of my statement caused my eyes to water, but I didn't let her see it.

"Ve better go to bed, honey," she said softly, caressing my cheek -- something I had never allowed her to do before.

"All right," I agreed, "Thank you for helping me with my book."

"You velcome. You know I have no pleasure in my life, but to help you."

"Yes," I said reluctantly. It has always been hard for me to accept love from her. Her moments of anger and her venomous words that left a deep scar, flashed before me. "God punished me when I conceived you! You were a curse from the beginning!" That was a moment of anger, and there were others similar, before and after. That was then. Today was different. None of that mattered anymore.

We hugged, but not as emotionally as I wished to have. I

needed more.

"Good night," I mumbled awkwardly, stalling in her arms for just another moment. I wanted to say more, oh, *so much more,* but I couldn't. I knew *she* would not be able to forget the past. It will always be an invisible wall between us. I had to be content in the knowledge of my own healing, and pray for hers.

*chapter twenty-one*

# Set Free

**The confrontation I had** with Mother two years before was the healing of my ugly attitude toward her, however instilled it was. Still left within me, was a desperate need which I conveniently ignored. But God has His ways.

I had been writing about God's character through the Hebrew meanings of some of His titles, one of which was *El Shaddai. El Shaddai* so aptly described the mother side of Him that I became supernaturally attracted to this part of God. In my mind I understood what He was showing me, and wrote it down. I knew someday I would be sharing these insights with others. One day, in the middle of writing, I was overcome with insecurity. *I can't write when I feel like this!* I complained to the Lord, and I pushed my writing aside. God's "sword," was skillfully slitting open my prickly pear skin.

Feeling exposed, I collapsed to my knees crying, "Lord, I feel so unloved, so alone, so deserted." I wept over the terror-filled abandonment of long ago as scene by scene it ripped through my heart. It was as if from a perpetual rickety crib -- as an adult toddler -- I am still screaming for comfort. I could bear it no longer! Deep from my innermost being, almost involuntarily, the words suddenly gushed out, "Oh God, El Shaddai, I need a mother right now!" I surprised myself, that I could be so candid, transparent before God. Instantly, I was overwhelmed with comforting peace -- a soothing balm at last to my life-long open wound. I saw that the horrid experience of abandonment prevailed upon my thoughts, my emotions, my behavior and view of people all my life. Tormenting surges of feeling forever unloved and forever uncomforted made me half a person. I also saw now that the lack of a mother had left a humanly unfillable vacuum -- a childhood need unfulfilled; a longing unattainable. Consciously, I let go of both my need and my longing for her love, and transferred it to my need of and desire for God. From God, love *is* attainable. Now I felt myself being thrusted upon Him. Unconsciously, I had crossed my arms across the shoulders, rocking as I sat on the floor, immersed in God's healing arms.

"El Shaddai," I repeated in perfect peace, calling on God's Motherly heart, "El Shaddai, I feel whole; I feel loved. You are my All." What I had been writing about by His instruction became my experience: God was not merely Father, but "mother," or "brother," or "aunt." Anyone I lack, He is to me. He has become the turner of my weakness into strength. After getting to know God as my El Shaddai and yielding to the "cutting," He healed my need. Did I have something to write about now!

Never since have I felt that awful vacuum. I learned that

it is better to give life to a deeper relationship with God than to mourn and miss a non-existing human relationship. How well I know the feeling; how much I appreciate the difference! I know God placed Himself in this "mother" vacuum, because that relationship never existed for me.

God had been working on my prickly skin. At the same time, He has been maturing the once stunted fruit inside. At first, it was as if He stood by a cart full of prickly pears and picked me up from the heap. Then, through a series of bittersweet experiences, the master healer, with lightning speed, took the two-edged sword of His Word and slit open my skin, and I was exposed. That was the bitter part, yet, the more I yielded to His "cutting," the more attention I received from Him. I thought that fair. As I got to really know God, He became a true *Parent* to me. That changed my orphan mentality. As I allowed Him to know me, He became a true *Friend*, and taught me to be less afraid of myself. This has been the experience of my whole person, the sweet part.

Daily, I must be immersed in Him, "dunked" in His Spirit afresh, without rushing away to join some traditional pattern, be it Jewish or Christian. Then He can teach me about Himself, His true character, and about me -- who I am; who I should become. The "Word" did not become the "Sword" until the revelation of **who He really is** cut deep into my innermost being. This is not a mere "inner healing" but what I prefer to call *innermost healing,* where the very core of me was transformed.

I have found it impossible to experience God this way without experiencing miraculous inner change -- change of character, and of personality. God changed my mindset, through "renewal of the mind," helping me to see and to understand life's circumstances from His point of view.

If we have been robbed of a natural relationship, intimate relationship with God is more than sufficient. "My grace is sufficient for thee: for my strength is made perfect in weakness" (II Corinthians 12:9). It truly is, but only if we let the Holy Spirit thrust us upon God, El Shaddai.

It matters not how much or what I suffered, or that I suffered at all. It matters only that I continually learn to change my mental outlook of a limited God, to that of my All, and to go on to a more mature life in Him. This is what makes me no longer the victim of my past, with every circumstance and every person affecting who I am. God Himself makes me the victor over it, and thus, I am permanently set free.

There is no counsel like the true counsel of God. There is no comfort like His healing arms. There is no restoration of the soul outside of Him -- alone with Him.

I still have a prickly skin, but its new spines no longer serve as self-protection from people. They are spiritual spines, serving to ward off the darts of the "accuser." God found a better use for my prickly exterior. He did not take it away, but merely taught me to use it more wisely, for Him.

Shriveled little pear that I was, God, tenderly but firmly, made me grow and become useful -- a true Sabra for God -- His prickly pear.

# BOOK ORDER / INFORMATION REQUEST FORM

## Intimate Awe Publications, P.O. Box 2283, Greeneville TN 37744

Orders for one book must include $1.50 to cover postage and handling. Postage is **FREE** for orders of **TWO** books or more. For bulk purchases call the toll free number below. Prices subject to change without notice.

Name _____

Address _____

City _____ State _____

_____ ZIP _____

_____ Book(s) x $10.95 ea. _____

Sales tax ( TN residents _____

Postage (if applicable) _____

Total $ _____

Method of payment: _____ Check or Money Order
_____ Credit card by mail
_____ Credit card by phone   **Toll Free (800) 722-7235**
_____ Please complete this form before you call.

Card Type: _____ Visa _____ Master Card   Number: _____

Expiration Date ___ / ___   Signature _____

## Please send me the items checked below:

_____ I would like to receive a current list of cassette tapes of Yaffa's teachings.

_____ I would like to be on your mailing list and receive notification when other books by Yaffa come into print.

_____ I would like to know more about Intimate Awe Ministries